Alex Crawford

Gloster Gladiator Vol 2

The Survivors in Detail

STRATUS

1

Published in Poland in 2011
by STRATUS s.c.
Po. Box 123,
27-600 Sandomierz 1, Poland
e-mail: office@mmpbooks.biz
for
Mushroom Model Publications,
3 Gloucester Close,
Petersfield
Hampshire GU32 3AX, UK.
e-mail: rogerw@mmpbooks.biz

ISBN
978-83-89450-64-7

Editor in chief
Roger Wallsgrove

Editorial Team
Bartłomiej Belcarz
Artur Juszczak
James Kightly
Robert Pęczkowski

Colour Drawings
Chris Sandham-Bailey

3D Drawings
Marek Ryś

Scale Plans
Dariusz Karnas

DTP
Robert Pęczkowski

Printed by
Drukarnia Diecezjalna,
ul. Żeromskiego 4,
27-600 Sandomierz
www.wds.pl
marketing@wds.pl

PRINTED IN POLAND

Table of Contents

Acknowledgement 3
Bibliography 4
Introduction 5
Gladiator Survivors 6
by James Kightly 6
Gladiator Mk II N5641 6
Gladiator Mk II N5579 7
Sea Gladiator Mk I N5520 (or N5519) 7
Gloster J8A C.No. G5/59066 Fv278 9
Gloster Gladiator Mk I (later Mk II) K8042 9
Gloster Gladiator Mk II N5628 10
Viv Bellamy's Gladiators 11
Gloster Gladiator Mk.l L8032 (G-AMRK) 11
Gloster Gladiator Mk II N5903 (G-GLAD) 12
Jet Age and Retro Gladiators 13
Aircraft maintenance and handling 16
Gloster Gladiator Technical Data 29
Scale plans 38
Gladiator in Detail 49
Gladiator in Detail: Fuselage 54
Gladiator in Detail: Wing 62
Gladiator in Detail: Canopy 72
Gladiator in Detail: Cockpit 74
Gladiator in Detail: Engine 89
Gladiator in Detail: Tail 96
Gladiator in Detail: Undercarriage 98
Gladiator in Detail: Armament 103
Swedish J8A in Detail 107
3D Anaglyph Images 113
Colour Profiles 119

***Title Page:** Gloster Gladiator Mk I (later Mk II) K8042 at The RAF Museum, Hendon. (Rob Leigh)*

Acknowledgement

During the 25 years I have researched the Gloster Gladiator I have had help from various groups, associations and literally hundreds of individuals. I would like to thank the following for all their help with this 2nd edition. They are in no particular order.

Australian Department of Defence, Sqn Ldr Paul Shepherd, Birger Larsen, John Gong, Ian Simpson, Robert R Brown, Joel Kuusman, Juha Vaittinen, Martti Kujansuu, Peter Holloway, Sally Ainslie, Sid Napier, Tore Eggan, Peter G Rackliff, Kari Stenman, Brian Cull, Andy Ingham, Lars Qvardfordt, Lennert Berns, Ted Burnett (Swedish Air Force Special Interest Group), P Cuthbert (3 Squadron RAAF Association), Dimitrios Filaos, Magnus Fridsall, Mark E Horan, LCDR Graham Horne (Curator 3RAAF Association, Aviation Museum of Western Australia), Ian Johnson (Hong Kong Historical Aircraft Association), Ossi Juntunen, Karl Kössler, D Y Louie, Ketil Lunde (Bodo Historical Aviation Society), Sergeant Eddie MalCullach (PR Section Irish Air Corps), Bob Massey, Nick Millman, V J Milner (Rigger, 615 Sqn), Blake Pelly (3 RAAF Gladiator pilot), James Pickering (Gladiator pilot), Major Kalevi Reinman (Finnish Air Force Headquarters), Yuri M Svoyski, Michel Terlinden, Arvo L Vercamer and Joao M Vidal.

To all those others that have helped with information and photos my deepest thanks.

Gloster Gladiator N5770 with side panels removed, 1940. (Author's coll.)

Bibliography

Books

Wg Cdr J Watson and L Jones , 3 RAAF Squadron at War, 3 Squadron Association.

May Brian Cull ,12 Days in May: The Air Battle for Northern France and the Low Countries, 10-21, Grub Street, London, 1999. (ISBN 1902304128)

605 Squadron by Ian Piper, Louis Drapkin Ltd, 2003. (ISBN 0952951614)

A Brief History of No3 Squadron RAAF 1916-46, (Authors unknown).

Aces High by Christopher Shores and Clive Williams, Grub Street, London, 1994. (ISBN 1898697000)

Aces High Vol 2 by Christopher Shores, Grub Street , London, 1999. (ISBN 1898697000)

Ace of Aces: M T St J Pattle by E C R Baker, Crecy Publishing, Cheshire, 1994. (ISBN 094755436X)

Air War for Yugoslavia, Greece and Crete 1940-41 by Christopher Shores, Grub Street, London, 1993. (ISBN 0948817070)

Carrier Fighters by David Brown, MacDonald and Janes, London.

Desert Air War 1939-45 by Richard Townshend Bickers, Pen & Sword Books / Leo Cooper, London, 1991. (ISBN 0850522161)

Desert Wings by Peter Holloway, Melverly Publishing 2001. (ISBN 0954188403)

Dust Clouds in the Middle East by Christopher Shores, Grub Street, London, 1996. (ISBN 189869737X)

Englantilaiset Havittajat by Keskinen, Stenman and Niska, Soumen Ilmavoimien Historia No12.

Famous Fighters of the Second World War by William Green, MacDonald, London.

Finnish Air Force in the Winter War by Keskinen and Stenman.

Fledgling Eagles by Christopher Shores, Grub Street, London, 1991. (ISBN 0948817429)

Fleet Air Arm Aircraft 1939-45 by Ray Sturtivant, (Air Britain (Historians) Ltd., 1998. (ISBN 0851302327)

From Bleriot to Spitfire by David Ogilvy, Airlife, 1991

Gladiators over Malta; The story of Faith, Hope and Charity by Brian Cull and Frederick Galea, Wise Owl Publications 2008. (ISBN 9789993292784)

Gloster Aircraft since 1917 by Derek N James, Putnam Aeronautical Books, 1987. (ISBN 0851778070)

Gloster Gladiator by Francis K Mason, MacDonald Aircraft Monographs, MacDonald, London.

Gloster Gladiator Aces by Andrew Thomas, Osprey Publishing Ltd. (ISBN 184176289X)

Gloster Gladiator in Action by W A Harrison, Squadron Signal Publications. (ISBN 0897474503)

Gloster Gladiator Warpaint by Tom Spencer, Warpaint Books Ltd. (ISSN 13610369)

Hurricanes over Tobruk: The Pivotal Role of the Hurricane in the Battle for Toburk, Western Desert, January-June 1941 by Brian Cull, Grub Street, London, 1999. (ISBN 190230411X)

Irish Gladiators by Patrick J Cummins.

Japanese Naval Aces and Fighter Aircraft in WWII by I Hato and Y Izawa, Airlife Books / Naval Institute Press, 1989. (ISBN 0870213156)

K File, RAF of the 1930's by James J Halley, MBE, Air Britain Publication, 1995.(ISBN 0851302246

Latvian Air Force 1918-1940, Insignia Air Force Special, Blue Rider Publishing. (ISBN 1902851048)

Lithuanian Air Force 1918-1940, Insignia Air Fore Special, Blue Rider Publishing. (ISSN 13604856)

Malta: The Hurricane Years 1940-41 by Christopher Shores, Brian Cull, and Nicola Malizia, Grub Street, London, 1990. (ISBN 0948817062)

Monografie Lotnicze No. 24 Gloster Gladiator by B Belcarz and R Peczkowski, AJ Press.

Norwegian Gladiators, (Authors unknown).

Prelude to Pearl Harbour by Ray Wagner, San Diego Aerospace Museum.

RAF Aircraft L1000-N9999 by James J Halley, Air Britain (Historians) Ltd, 1993. (ISBN 0851302084)

RAF Fighter Command Claims of World War Two: Vol 1 1939-1940 by John Foreman, Red Kite, 2003. (ISBN 0953806189)

RAF Fighter Command Losses of the Second World War: Volume 1 by N L Franks, Midland Publishing, Leicester, 1997. (ISBN 1857800559)

Royal Air Force The Aircraft in Service Since 1918 by Michael Turner, Temple Press 1981

South African Air Force at War by Martin Louw and Stefan Bouwer.

Spitfires over Israel by Brian Cull, Shlomo Aloni and David Nicolle, Grub Street, London, 1993.

Springbok Fighter Victory, SAAF Fighter Operations 1939-1945, Vol 1 East Africa 1940-1941 by Michael Schoeman, Freeworld Publications CC, 2002. (ISBN 0958438854)

Strike True, The story of 80 Squadron RAF by Christopher Shores, Air Britain Publication. (ISBN 0851301266)

The War That Never Was by Air Vice Marshall A G Dudgeon, Airlife Publishing, Shrewsbury, 1991. (ISBN 1853102563)

Those Other Eagles by Christopher Shores, Grub Street, London, 2004.(ISBN 1904010881)

Twenty One Squadrons; The history of the Royal Auxiliary Air Force 1925-1957 by Leslie Hunt, Crecy, 1992. (ISBN 0947554262)

Wings of the Weird & Wonderful by Eric Brown, Airlife 1983

Wings over Ireland: The Story of the Irish Air Corps by Donald MacCarron, Midland Publishing, 1996. (ISBN 1857800575)

Magazines and journals

Aeroplane Monthly, various issues.

Aero Journal, Vol. 12 and Vol. 14.

Air Enthusiast, various issues.

Air Pictorial, various issues.

Avions, various issues.

IPMS Millari No. 32. IPMS Finland.

Malta Flypast issue no. 2.

Pilot Magazine, May 2000

Small Air Forces Observer, various issues.

Wings - Encyclopaedia of Aviation. Orbis Publishing

Web sites

Gloster Gladiator by Alex Crawford
http://www.geocities.com/acrawford0/

Malta's Sea Gladiators by Richard Caruana
http://www.faasig.org/colors/malta.htm

Rick Kent's Profiles
Camouflage and Markings of Gloster Gladiator
http://www.hotel.wineasy.se/ipms/stuff_eng_profile_gladiator1.htm

Håkans aviation page
Biplane Fighter Aces from the Second World War
http://www.dalnet.se/~surfcity/index.html

Gloster Gladiator in Detail
http://www.hotel.wineasy.se/ipms/stuff_eng_detail_gladiator.htm

The Jet Age Museum, Gloucestershire
http://www.jetagemuseum.org/

The Fighter Collection's Gladiator
http://www.avnet.co.uk/tfc/gladiator/

Introduction

This second volume covers the technical side of the Gloster Gladiator. With a mass of photos the 'bare bones' of the aircraft is laid bare for all to see. Each aircraft was hand built in a section of the workshop. The Gladiator was probably one of the last British aircraft to be built this way before the mass production of WWII came into being. As a result a part from one aircraft didn't always fit another aircraft as the locating holes were drilled by hand. A full maintenance description is given and it shows how much attention was required to keep these aircraft in the air.

Also included, and possibly a first for any aviation book are a number of 3D drawings showing various parts of the airframe. These drawings have been specially commissioned for this book. Additional photos and colour side view drawings are also included and provide further camouflage details of the various units that flew the Gladiator.

The Shuttleworth Collection's Gladiator G-AMRK, for many years the only flying example, taxies out for another display in 2008. (A. Juszczak)

Gladiator Survivors

by James Kightly

When the first edition of this book was published, there was a number of complete airframes, wrecks and only one flyer, which had been the sole airworthy example for decades. At the time of writing, there are now two airworthy examples in the UK, and another on the way, albeit long term. Additionally there are a number more restorations which will deliver more Gladiators to public view.

Back in 1974, according to Leslie Hunt's Veteran & Vintage Aircraft, there were eight known airframes; the airworthy G-AMRK (L8032) with The Shuttleworth Collection, then single machines in Malmen, Sweden, No.278; Dovre, Norway (N5579 - previously thought to be N5641) stored substantially complete in a purpose-built shed. The famous N5519 in the Palace Armoury, Malta and N5589 in Wildenrath, West Germany, with Fit Lt Jeremy Collins of 60 Squadron which had been recovered from Lake Lesjakog, Norway. In England was N5903, dismantled at Yeovilton, on loan from The Shuttleworth Collection, awaiting restoration; while the RAF Museum had N5628's fuselage and engine remains, again recovered from Lake Lesjakog, as well as the complete K8042.

Gladiator Mk II N5641

Today there is no significant change in the number of machines, but the muddied Norwegian machines turned out to be both airframes – the substantially complete one rescued in 1940, and preserved by local man Ludvig Hope, turned out to be N5641, and is today Bodo, fully restored to static condition, suspended in its original colours HE-G of 263 Squadron.

Gladiator Mk II N5641 in the Norsk Luftfartsmuseum *(Norwegian Aviation Museum) in Bodo fully restored in 263 Squadron colours. (via P. Skulski)*

Gladiator Mk II N5579 seen in the restoration facility at the Fleet Air Arm Museum, Yeovilton. (J. Kightly)

Gladiator Mk II N5579

Gladiator N5579 was intended to be a static restoration project in Norway, but passed, via the Jet Age Museum, Staverton, to the Fleet Air Arm Museum, Yeovilton, the restored fuselage (illustrated) being handed over in July 2002 and the whole aircraft intended to be reconstructed as Sea Gladiator "Royal Navy N5518".

Sea Gladiator Mk I N5520 (or N5519)

The most evocative of the partial airframes is the Sea Gladiator on Malta. The sole genuine surviving Sea Gladiator, it is a machine with an air of mystery, and the heavy restorations (separate laudable but under-resourced efforts on at least three occasions) makes it no easier to decipher the machine's real story. Is it N5519 (the aircraft given as the machine shot down in flames?) or N5520? Was it one of the flying machines, or a cannibalised airframe?

What is certain is that the aircraft was recovered from a quarry at Kalafrana, presented to the people of Malta (and represented as the Gladiator 'Faith') by Air Vice Marshal Sir Keith Park in 1943, after which it resided in the Palace Armoury until 1973. It was then transferred to The National War Museum, Fort St Elmo, where it rests to this day. What was recovered from the quarry was a minimal airframe, standing on tyreless wheels, and consisting of the fuselage, lower centre section, and tail feathers, excluding the rudder. For its presentation an engine and two-bladed wooden propeller were found and fitted, and later some fabric work, an inaccurately shaped rudder and a cowling (with oversize cylinder head teardrops) were attached, which is how it appears today.

Over the years various parties have tried to prove on the one hand that this was one of the 'three' and definitely "Faith' while on the other hand various other authorities have cast doubt on if the aircraft had ever flown or was just a cannibalised airframe. There are marks on the wing attachments consistent with the wings being fitted at some point: the undercarriage is bent, consistent with a minor landing mishap, and it has the locally invented armour headrest. The machine is painted as N5520, though many sources have it as N5519. and most of the serial numbers were filed off at some point – one can only presume to fudge the full identification of the machine. On the refit in 1973, the serial N5520 was discovered on the lower fuselage fairing aft of the tailwheel. Does this prove to be a serial missed by the people trying to hide the i.d. of the machine, or is it a very useful discovery to be found? As ever, there is evidence to support whichever presumption is wanted. Either way, the aircraft usefully acts as a symbol of the saga.

However, this is not the end of the story. Ray Polidano, the Director of the MAM brings us up to date:

"The story of the fuselage of N5520 being transferred from the National War Museum in Valletta to the Aviation Museum Ta'Qali started in 1996 when Minister Michael Refalo, then Minister of Justice and Arts suggested and promised financial support for the construction of wings for 'Faith'. With the construction of wings for 'Faith' one would assume that, there being no space for the complete aircraft at the War Museum, the aircraft would be moved to the Aviation Museum Ta'Qali. In 1997, the British High Commissioner G.R Archer wrote on our behalf to the Trustees of the Keeper of the Collections Division at the Royal Air Force Museum if they would consider donating wing parts held by them so that these parts would be used for the complete restoration of 'Faith'. The wing parts were donated to the Aviation Museum in September 1998 and they were accepted on behalf of the Aviation Museum by The Hon. Dr Louis Galea, Minister of Education and National Culture.

In the meantime the Aviation Museum also acquired three pieces of Gladiator wings from Suomen Ilmailumuseo (The Finnish Aviation Museum). Unfortunately, since that time, here in Malta we had several change of Governments and corresponding Ministers, all with different point of views on what should happen to 'Faith'. In 1996, we were dealing with The Museums Department, who supported our initiative to set up an Aviation Museum on Malta (Malta, up to 1996, must have been the only state in Europe, or indeed most of the World, not to have an Aviation Museum). Now we are dealing with

Malta's enigmatic and iconic Sea Gladiator fuselage seen in 2002. (J. Kightly)

Heritage Malta (The equivalent of the National Trust in UK) who are totally opposed to the transfer of 'Faith' to the Aviation Museum. They refer to 'Faith' as an Archeological Artifact and regard any restoration of aircraft as breaking the museums code. The present Minister of Culture had stated publicly that he was in favour of 'Faith' moving to the Aviation Museum but so far has done nothing about it. In conclusion, the situation now is to wait and see."

Gloster J8A Fv278 on show in the Flygvapenmuseum *(Swedish Air Force Museum) Linköping. (M. Shreeve)*

Gloster J8A C.No. G5/59066 Fv278

Delivered to Sweden in 1938 as Fv278, this machine is displayed in the colours it wore from January to March 1940 when flying with the Swedish volunteer group attached to the Finnish Air Force, fighting the Russians. Given that this machine was donated as early as 1940 to the Royal Swedish Air Force Collection with whom it has remained ever since, either stored or on display, it is certainly the most authentic of the surviving airframes; albeit the Mark II export version.

Gloster Gladiator Mk I (later Mk II) K8042

K8042, which acquired the maintenance serial No 8272M when used as an instructional airframe, was originally modified (probably) by Marshall's of Cambridge for meteorological use. This machine was built as a Mk I, later upgraded to Mk II standard, and then serving at A & AEE

The RAF Museum's Gladiators - Above: K8042, in the Battle of Britain Hall, lower: the remains of Gladiator Mk II N5628. (Both R. Pęczkowski)

Boscombe Down. It passed through Biggin Hill and later storage at Henlow, before becoming one of the original machines installed upon the opening of the RAF Museum in 1972. Later, with the opening of the Battle of Britain Hall, it was moved there in 1978, and this is where it remains today. Interestingly it has at least one modification from standard, being fitted with windscreen de-icing kit - perhaps an adoption from its period as a Met Flight aircraft?

Gloster Gladiator Mk II N5628

There is another Gladiator relic at Hendon, which is the forward fuselage recovered by the RAF Sub-Aqua Club in 1970 and displayed there as a contrast to the more complete airframes, and as a memorial to the disastrous Norwegian campaign.

Remains of Gladiator Mk II N5628 at Hendon. (Dariusz Karnas)

Viv Bellamy's Gladiators

The histories of the word's only flying Gladiators are inextricably entwined, so we begin this part by considering L8032 and N5903 together. In 1951 Viv Bellamy of Flightways chanced upon the two Gladiators held in store by Air Service Training, after they had been abandoned by Glosters when the planned conversion to meteorological flight duties was rendered unnecessary. Viv had flown Gladiators during the war, and was able to obtain both aircraft for £10. He then set about getting one into the air. The engine from N5903 (a Mercury VIIIAS) was only eight hours old, but the airframe of L8032 (originally rolled out from Brockworth on the 4th of October 1938) was in better nick, so the engine was transferred to L8032 and with the Watts two-bladed propeller of L8032's Mercury IX. Registered as G-AMRK, painted in black upon the overall silver scheme it took to the air again on the evening of the 13th of June 1952 at Eastleigh. This set the pattern for the next half century, with L8032 flying on almost without break, and the Cinderella, N5903, providing the odd part when L8032 needed it. Both were sold back to Glosters for £200 pounds by Viv in 1953; the sale being forced by the paucity of possible airshow bookings in the era.

Back with Glosters, the enthusiastic workforce were able to restore the machine to military colours plus completing a deep overhaul between 1955 and 1958 when G-AMRK reappeared as 'K8032', the false 'K' prefix being chosen as more contemporary than 'L' for a pre-war 72 Sqn machine. The apprentices who undertook the work added the four guns, the proper spade-grip was re-added, and a TR9 radio. Glosters were not to survive into the sixties, and the machine was thus donated to The Shuttleworth Collection, by then known as the home for such machines, in November 1960.

Gloster Gladiator Mk.I L8032 (G-AMRK)

At Old Warden ever since 1967, G-AMRK has been maintained continuously in airworthy condition, except when under refurbishment, like most of the Shuttleworth machines, this is a unique challenge. By 1971 another proper overhaul was needed, and Flight One at Staverton Airport were

The world's only airworthy Gladiators as seen on the Duxford flightline in 2008. (J. Kightly)

Shuttleworth's Gladiator rolls out on landing at Old Warden. (A. Juszczak)

contracted to renew ail the fabric and check the airframe. On this inspection it was discovered that the port upper wing was doped in a Sea Gladiator scheme, and the part number was from an entirely separate batch, indicating that this mainplane had indeed come from this type. The Mercury VIII was worn out by 1986 and was thus replaced with a Mercury XXX (30). During this period of the late eighties and early nineties, the Gladiator was sponsored by Luton Airport - in recognition of the fact that a flight of Gladiators had helped 'open' the original airport. In 1990 a groundloop bent the port axle stub out of alignment, and again N5903 provided a replacement. In 1975 the false 'K' was replaced with the correct 'L'. and the 72 Sqn colours were retained until 1990 when a 'temporary' Battle of Britain scheme (247 Squadron, as 'N2308') was applied giving a whole new look before the fabric was completely replaced. The anticipated wear of the camouflage overpaint did not occur, but the replacement of the fabric was still needed. Norwegian TV wanted to feature a flying Gladiator in a documentary on the wartime story, and so L8032 was painted once again in silver, but this time with the unusual and attractive Norwegian Air Force wing and tail flashes. Another repaint in 2007 saw it enter another pre-war RAF scheme as K7985 of 73 Squadron RAF, as was flown by 'Cobber' Kain at the 1937 Hendon Air Pageant. A balance between very conservative but expressive flying (it is currently cleared to undertake limited acrobatics) and husbanding the scarce spares has kept this in the air, giving pleasure to thousands, and existing as a jewel in the collection's crown.

Gloster Gladiator Mk II N5903 (G-GLAD)

The Shuttleworth Collection generously lent N5903 to the Fleet Air Arm Museum at Yeovilton; where the incomplete airframe was restored to static condition, and partially mocked-up in Sea Gladiator configuration by a team of volunteers. This was a laudably well undertaken job, as the engine, propeller, spinner and flaps were missing, as well as many other parts which had been used

on L8032. In 1994 Shuttleworth sold the machine to The Fighter Collection for rebuild to airworthy condition; which job commenced as soon as the aircraft was transported to Duxford, and where it was registered G-GLAD and finally flew again in 2008 finally emerging from the shadow of L8032 and back in the air, in 72 Squadron pre-war colours.

On a test flight early in its new flying career, the Fighter Collection's Gladiator N5903. (J. Kightly)

Jet Age and Retro Gladiators

Tim Kershaw fills in the details of the Cotswold Gladiators:

"The Jet Age Museum and Retro Track and Air have now collaborated on four Gladiator rebuild projects. They are largely based on wreckage of aircraft of 263 Squadron RAF, lost during the second Norwegian expedition in 1940, recovered by Jet Age members over the last few years and gifted to the museum by the Norwegian government. Jet Age member Don Tombs, a former Gloster Aircraft Company draughtsman, has produced a large number of new drawings based on damaged original components and Jet Age and Retro have also had access to surviving original Gloster drawings.

Three more Jet Age members, Brian Walker, Bill Jeffrey and Will Moore, make up the restoration team at Retro's premises at Cam, near Dursley, Gloucestershire. Their first reconstruction was a basic fuselage for the Norwegian Air Force Museum. It is based on original parts from more than one crash site, has no identity and will be united with the original wings and tail unit of a Norwegian Air Force Gladiator to make a representative aircraft. The Norwegian wings and tail unit are currently on loan to Retro as patterns for N5719/G-CBHO (see below). The completed fuselage frame is stored at Kemble and will go to Norway with the wings and tail when they are returned.

The same team has rebuilt another basic fuselage for the Fleet Air Arm Museum at Yeovilton. Again, it was built from an assortment of original parts and has no identity, although it is expected to be completed as the sole Fleet Air Arm Gladiator to serve in Norway.

Jet Age Museum's own Gladiator rebuild is N5914, in which P/O J.I. Wilkie of 263 Squadron RAF died on 2 June 1940 when he was shot down over Lille Haugefjell by the German ace Helmut Lent. It will consist largely of original parts as Jet Age was able to recover most of the wreckage from the mountain. The complex tail bay of the fuselage has been restored and the main frame from the pilot's seat forward is nearly complete in its jig, including a cross-tube with original bullet hole. The engine is reasonably complete, although corroded.

The front fuselage structure has been dismantled from the build jig for treatment/painting prior to final assembly. Jet Age Gladiator team leader Brian Walker says that this structure has demanded a greater number of hours of labour than that of the previous frames, i.e. those of Yeovilton and Norway respectively. Several components had to be substantially refurbished, fabricated, or newly manufactured, most needing some careful thought as to alternative ways of production. Significant challenges yet to be addressed are the restoration of a pair of undercarriage legs, as is the provisioning of the full complement of fuselage bracing wires.

A fourth Gladiator, N5719, is being rebuilt to fly by Retro's own team as a flying aircraft. The main fuselage frame is complete and work is well advanced on the port lower wing and on the restoration of an original Mercury engine. N5719 was flown by P/O M.A. Craig-Adams of 263 Squadron RAF, who was killed in action on 22 May 1940 over Hogfjellet. He flew into the side of a mountain and his body was eventually recovered by French troops in 1945. The civil registration G-CBHO has already been allocated and Retro is looking for an investment partner to complete the project. At Retro's own website at www.retrotrackandair.com, there are photographs by Richard Winslade showing progress to date.

The Jet Age Museum was able to acquire other Gladiator parts when the RAF Museum's reserve collection was moved from Cardington to Stafford. The RAF Museum parts were mostly from 263 Squadron's first Norwegian expedition and were recovered from Lake Lesjaskog. The Gladiator wings and tail from Cardington went to Malta. Jet Age proposed that most of the other parts should go to Yeovilton in exchange for their support for their application to the Norwegian government to recover wreckage from the second Norwegian expedition. Jet Age received engine parts, a burnt wooden propeller and a number of other small components, including some parts from N5628, the forward fuselage of which is an exhibit at the RAF Museum.

(A. Juszczak)

(A. Juszczak)

Aircraft maintenance and handling

The following is a translation of a Swedish manual for the Gladiator J8/8A. The manual for the RAF machines would be very similar apart from the extra maintenance carried out to the Swedish Gladiators during winter operations.

The aircraft's correct handling and maintenance are very important for keeping the aircraft in good condition, operational and to keep up its good performance. For this it is mandatory that the aircraft is taken care of and that any possible exceptions made from the maintenance instructions due to special circumstances, lack of time and weather conditions are carefully considered carefully beforehand with expertise.

Instructions on handling the aircraft

Flight instructions

All combat manoeuvres can be done with this aircraft except for a back tailspin and an inverted loop. During flight the following limitations should be taken into account:

Maximum allowed speed when brake flaps are open is 160 km/h

Maximum allowed dive speed is 480 km/h

Maximum allowed rpm in a dive is 3120 rpm.

For using the fuel cocks, mixture lever etc. the following instructions are to be followed.

Before a flight the pilot must make sure (from the mechanic and fuel gauge) that there is enough fuel in the tank. The gravity tank must be full even before short flights. The take off and flight should be done with main tank. The gravity tank is for emergencies only.

Before each flight the pilot must make sure the throttle and all other levers' friction holders locking screws are tight enough. The locking screws should not be tightened so the levers are unusable.

Before takeoff the mixture lever should be pulled far back, past the stopper groove, so the manifold pressure restriction device begins to operate. After this the throttle is pushed full forwards, so the maximum power can be achieved during takeoff.

Line up of the Swedish Gloster Gladiators. Note the underwing bomb racks. (Archive Svensk Flyghistirisk Förening)

When the manifold pressure (as the mixture lever is in the far back position as described above) is dropped to a level of 0 gr/cm^2 the mixture lever should be returned to its normal position (to the stopper groove).

Type characteristics

Speed
The most efficient speed for climb = 195 km/h.
Normal glide with brake flaps extended = 125 km/h.
Take off speed = 95 km/h
Landing speed = 80-85 km/h

Take off and landing distances
Take off distance without exceeding manifold pressure time limit = approx 225 m.
With exceeded manifold pressure time limit = approx 200 m.

Landing distance:
Without brakes = approx 300 m.
With brakes = approx 175 m.

Stabiliser settings
Cruising rpm +2.5° or 3°
During glide (125 – 130 km/h) ± 0°
Landing -1° or -1.5°
Changing engine rpm or opening the brake flaps does not significantly alter the aircraft stability.

Dives
During a dive, while engine is set to idle the speed versus rpm should be according to the following:
440 km/h at 2650 rpm
460 km/h at 2900 rpm

Inverted flight
The aircraft is easily controlled in an inverted flight. During the pull up, which occurs at approx 130 km/h speed range, the aircraft tilts fairly slowly. The aircraft does not have any tendency to go in a tailspin.

Loading instructions
It is strictly forbidden to exceed the aircraft's maximum allowed take off weight (see aircraft weight distribution).

Instructions and procedures before and after flight

Summer
Pre-flight procedures
Two litres of hot oil (50C°) is pressed into the engine with a pressure of 70 lbs/in^2 through the oil gauge connector located at the oil pump, if the aircraft has bee unused for 14 days or longer.

Hot oil is pressed into the supercharger from grease fittings in the rear end and backside of the crankcase if the engine has been unused for 5 days or longer.

Before starting the engine it is necessary to make sure that there is enough fuel and oil.

Check that there is enough fuel in the fuel primer. Normal fuel can be used in the primer.

Check that all control movement is free. Check that all hatches are closed and that all latches are properly locked.

Check, that tyre pressure in the main landing gear is correct and tail wheel.

Check that the oil level in the air compressor is correct (By pressing the valve on the lower backside of the compressor down until all excess oil has drained out).

Check that wheel brakes operate correctly.

Check that brake flaps operate correctly.

The engine pre warm up and testing is done according to the following:

The engine is operated for approximately 5 minutes with 700-800 rpm and after this for at least 5 minutes with 1000 rpm. The inner cooler units must be open at this time.

Check that:

Oil pressure is 3.5 – 4.2 kg/cm^2

Fuel pressure is 0.1 – 0.25 kg/cm^2 (Maximum pressure is 0.28 kg/cm^2).

When during the above mentioned engine warm up, the oil temperature has risen to 20 C^o the engine testing can be started.

During the engine testing, when the control stick has to be kept in the full back position, the following things should be checked:

Engine rpm with full throttle: approx 1800 rpm.

Mixture control in normal position and approx 1900 rpm.

Mixture control lever at time limited setting.

During testing the engine can be operated with full throttle for a maximum of 20 seconds.

The fuel pump pressure is 0.1 – 0.25 kg/cm^2 (Maximum pressure is 0.28 kg/cm^2).

Oil pressure is 4.2 kg/cm^2

Manifold pressure:

Mixture lever in normal position: approx +70 gr/cm^2.

Mixture control lever at time limited setting: approx +170 gr/cm^2.

The maximum permitted decrease of rpm when one magneto is disconnected is 60 rpm.

The Magneto testing is done with full throttle and 1250 – 1300 rpm.

The engine is stopped by turning the ignition switch to "0" position and after this the pull handle of the idling spray stopping valve is pulled until the engine goes to a halt. Before stopping the engine it should run idle for at least 1 minute.

Before starting the engine the intake air control lever is set to "cold" position. After the engine has been started the control lever is put to "warm" position and is kept here through the engine warm up. The engine testing is done with the lever in "cold" position and the plane is passed to the pilot, with the control in this position.

After engine testing the primer reservoir is filled (with normal fuel).

Procedures after flight

The aircraft oil tank is filled.

The fuel tanks (main- and fall tank) are filled and the strainer in the filler funnel is not damaged and is clean.

The fuel filter is cleaned.

The engine and aircraft are carefully cleaned.

The engine and aircraft are inspected.

If the aircraft is left out side the controls must be locked, cockpit canopy closed and the aircraft firmly secured to the ground.

Those points in the aircraft that require lubrication and greasing must be taken care of weekly.

Winter

Pre-flight procedures

Cylinders number 4, 5, 6 and 7 are drained from possibly accumulated oil.

The oil tank is filled with warm oil (50 – 70 C°).

Hot oil is pressed into the supercharger from grease fittings in the rear of the crankcase.

Hot oil is pressed into the engine (through the oil gauge connector located at the oil pump), simultaneously rotating the crankshaft from the propeller, immediately before starting up the engine.

Before starting the engine it is necessary to make sure that there is enough fuel.

The engine is started and the warm up and testing is done in the same manner as during the summer. In the winter the engine has to be primed more: 10 – 15 strokes. During warm up all oil coolers are kept closed. The engine testing is done with the inner oil cooler opened.

Procedures after flight

All oil from the tank, lines and engine is drained out when it is still warm.

The aircraft skis are overhauled.

Otherwise all is done the same as during the summer.

Routine checkups and maintenance procedures

Airframe

Daily inspections

Check:

That the airframe, wings and rudder fabric covering are not damaged in any way.

That the propeller is in good condition.

Upper view of the Swedish Gladiator, 8-41. (Archive Svensk Flyghistirisk Förening)

That the landing gear wheels are properly secured.

The landing gear tyres have normal pressure (approx. 3.4 kg/cm²) and that they are not damaged.

That the pressure in the landing gear system is normal (tested from the lever on the flight stick).

That the control stick and pedals have free movement to their extreme positions.

That the horizontal stabiliser adjustment mechanism works properly.

That the brake flaps mechanism works properly.

That the canopy can be moved freely backwards and forwards.

That the windshield cleaning system tank is filled.

That the safety belt is in good condition and their locking mechanism works properly.

That the windshields are intact; clean them and the anti-glare shields.

That the horizontal stabiliser and its tension wires are rigid.

That the vertical stabiliser, elevator and rudder are undamaged.

That the tail wheel is in good condition and the pressure is normal (1.8 – 2.0 kg/cm²).

That the wing tension wires are normal.

That the access covers are intact and firmly shut.

That the aircraft is clean inside and outside.

Inspections after every 10 hours of flight

In addition to the daily inspections the following procedures and inspections must be done after every 10 hours of flight.

Lubricate the landing gear wheels hubs (inner and outer grease fittings).

Check that the landing gear wheel fastening bolts are firmly secured.

Lubricate the pedal mechanism bearings.

Grease the control stick connecting rods front and rear ball bearing.

Grease the aileron control lever mechanism and elevator control wiring bearings behind the pilot seat.

Test that the stabiliser adjustment mechanisms friction device works properly.

Lubricate the horizontal stabiliser adjustment mechanism hand wheels shaft and indicating devices shaft.

Lubricate the cockpit side window latches.

Inspect that the horizontal stabiliser adjustment devices screw mechanism and chain wheel in the aft of the airframe are not worn. Lubricate the screw mechanism chain and chain wheel.

Lubricate and inspect the rudder hinges.

Inspect the rudder and elevators bearing supports flange and bolt connections.

J8 of the Swedish Air Force. (Archive Svensk Flyghistirisk Förening)

Close up photo of the J8 coded 8-45. Inter wing bracing is well visible. (Archive Svensk Flyghistirisk Förening)

Inspect the elevators bearing supports and lubricate the elevators hinges.

Lubricate the elevators mid bearing and the screw mechanism and horizontal stabilisers joints bearings. Lubricate the screw mechanism.

Lubricate the bearing points located at the horizontal stabiliser front spar.

Inspect the tail wheel assembly's fastenings.

Lubricate the tail wheel bearings.

Inspect the ailerons bearing mounts and lubricate the bearings.

Inspect the brake flaps and lubricate the bearings.

Inspection after every 20 hours of flight.

In addition to the daily inspections and the inspections after every 10 hours of flight the following procedures and inspections must be done after every 20 hours of flight.

Inspect that there is not excessive movement between the landing gear and wheels.

Inspect that the landing gear tires have normal pressure (approx. 3.4 kg/cm^2).

Add oil to the landing gear spring mechanism. Inspect the landing gear struts covering.

Test the brake system and verify that the brake band does not rub against the brake drum when not braking.

Test the pilot seat adjustment device has free movement and lubricate the adjustment device bearings. The adjustment device bearings located at the cross tubes are self lubricating.

Inspect that the wheel brake line fittings do not leak (the lines are then pressurised).

Empty the braking device oil separator and air filter.

Inspect that the firing mechanism flexible tubing is not worn at the bottom of the flight stick.

Inspect that the rudder control block on the control stick are not worn.

Inspect the rudder, elevator and horizontal stabiliser control wiring, giving special attention to places where the wiring goes through guides. Inspect that the wire locks, joints and fasteners are well secured.

Inspect the lower wing attachment bolts.

Inspect that the aileron control blocks on the control stick are not worn.

Inspect the elevator control mechanism idler.

Inspect the horizontal stabiliser front spar bolt assemblies.

Inspect the horizontal stabiliser rear spar bolt assemblies.

Inspect the vertical stabiliser attachment.

Inspect the horizontal stabiliser tension wiring fasteners.

Inspect the rudder movement control blocks.

Measure the oil level in the tail wheel shock strut and air pressure in the tyre (correct pressure is 1.8 – 2.0 kg/cm^2).

Inspect that the wing tension wiring crossing areas are not worn.

Inspect the tension wiring attachment points and verify that they well secured.

Inspect the streamline wire attachment points between the ailerons and verify that the wiring has correct tension when the control stick is centred.

Inspect the upper wing ailerons suspended position and verify the tension of the lower wing aileron control wiring through the inspection hatches at the bottom of the lower wing. The upper wing ailerons should drop 5 mm downwards when the lower wing ailerons are centred.

Inspect the wear of the aileron control mechanism (rudder levers forked end and the inner chain wheels connecting rods joint, located in the wings).

Verify that the aileron control wiring and chords are not worn, especially around the guides (only in lower wings).

Inspect the upper and lower wings bolted connections.

Fron view of the J8A. (Archive Svensk Flyghistirisk Förening)

Inspections after every 40 hours of flight

In addition to the daily inspections and the inspections after every 10 hours and 20 hours of flight the following procedures and inspections must be done after every 40 hours of flight.

Verify that the propeller does not wobble.
Inspect the propeller blades, hub and hub shape.
Remove the landing gear wheels outer hub covers and verify that the wheel bolts are properly tight.
Verify that the brake drum fastening bolts are properly tight.
Add oil to the landing gear wheel shock absorber if necessary.
Lubricate the pedals foot holder pivots.
Brake flap pump is filled with spindle oil.
Inspect the airframe fabric covering and inspection hatches.
Inspect the engine mounting ring and engine mount struts.
Inspect the exhaust collector.
Inspect the airframes aft part tension wires.
Verify that the rudder is in centre position when pedals are centred.
Verify that the elevator is in centre position when control stick is centred.
Inspect the tail light mounting.
Inspect the wing ribs and centre section ribs.
Inspect the wing leading and trailing edges.
Inspect the wing main ribs joints and tension wires inside wing.
Verify that brake flaps are not damaged and they do not have excess movement.

Inspections after every 120 hours of flight

In addition to the daily inspections and the inspections after every 10 hours 20 hours and 40 hours of flight_the following procedures and inspections must be done after every 120 hours of flight.

Remove landing gear wheels and check if the brake band and brake drum are not excessively worn.
Test the brake systems distribution valve functioning and lubricate the parts that ware.
Inspect that the brake systems lines are not damaged and the connectors are tight.
Inspect the airframe tubing for any change in shape and that their joints are not damaged.
Inspect the airframe formers and test that the tension wires are rigid enough.
Inspect the rudder and elevator bearings.
Check that the centre wing section supports are not bent.
Inspect the aileron bearings.
Inspect the aircraft trimming.

Powerplant

Inspections after every 10 hours of flight

Inspect the exhaust collector seams.

Inspect the engine collector tube attachments to the aircraft and the Townend rings attachment to the exhaust collector.

Lubricate the valve shafts and rocker arm adjustment screws (while engine is warm).
Clean the rocker arm mechanism parts that are uncovered and inspect the valve abrasion studs.
Check the valve clearance with a feeler gauge.
Check the oil level in the air compressor.
Inspect the throttle and mixture control mechanism and lubricate moving parts.
Fuel filter is removed and cleaned.
Oil filter is removed and cleaned.
Inspect the inlet air heat control mechanism.
Inspect that all nuts and bolts in the engine mount are tight, and secured.

Inspections after every 20 hours of flight

In addition to the inspections after every 10 hours of flight, the following procedures and inspections must be done after every 20 hours of flight.

Remove the valve rocker covers and inspect the valve stem and valve rockers.

Remove the valve rockers lubrication felts and soak them in approx 50°C oil for approx. one hour. (When removed, the pieces of felts should be kept in order, so to not mix them up). The felts inside the valve rocker covers are soaked in the same way.

Measure the angle between the valve rockers and valve stem, with a tool specially designed for this.

Check that the inlet air pipe joints are solid.

Test the compression in every cylinder.

Check that the throttle lever and mixture lever (in the carburettor) positions are correct.

Change the oil in the pneumatic appliance (wheel brake mechanism) oil tank. Before this procedure it is necessary to release the pressure in the lines.

Inspect the magneto and brake devices springs.

Measure the breaker point gap, check that the breakers move freely and that the points are clean and oil free.

Clean and inspect the ignition distributor and breaker covers and check that the electrical wiring is firmly attached and proper.

Check that the ignition distributors segments are clean and not corroded and that the breaker covers spring is intact.

Check that the magnetos work well and the electrical wiring is properly attached to the magnetos.

Clean the spark plug electrical wiring.

Clean the spark plugs, measure the gap and re-adjust if necessary. Test the sparkplugs at a pressure of 7 kg/cm^2.

The fuel feed line is removed from the carburettor and the fuel flow from the fall tank is verified.

Rinse the carburettor, clean the nozzles and check that they do not have any corrosion.

Check the fuel and oil lines.

Check the tubing joints and that thy do not at any point rub against anything.

Check the electric starter wiring.

Check that the engine control device joints do not have excessive movement or tightness and that the throttle and mixture control are set correctly.

Test that the fuel selection valves move freely and that they work as indicated in the panel.

Inspect the fuel tanks and their ventilation lines (one tube from gravity tank to the main tank and one tube from the main tank to the side of the airframe).

Inspections after every 40 hours of flight

In addition to the inspections after every 10 hours and 20 hours of flight the following procedures and inspections must be done after every 40 hours of flight.

Remove the propeller and inspect the hub and propeller shaft key piece and hub bolts.

Squeeze grease in to valve rocker bearings.

Check to see that valve push rods, valve rocker mount bolts and rocker arm axles do not have excessive clearance.

Inspect all engine electrical wiring.

Lubricate the magnetos.

Inspect the oil tank, empty the whole oil system (oil must be warm when doing this) and refill with clean oil.

Clean the oil tank strainer.

Inspect the primer pump and verify that the gasoline goes from the pump to the engine.

Inspect the magnetos ground wiring.

Check that all fuel lines are well protected against vibration by cushions between the brackets and fuel lines and that they can not start rubbing at any place.

Check the fuel tank mounting, and that the tank is free of corrosion.

Check the oil cooler joints.

Inspections after every 120 hours of flight

In addition to the inspections after every 10, 20, and 40 hours of flight the following procedures and inspections must be done after every 120 hours of flight.

Engine of the J8 with the cowling removed. (Archive Svensk Flyghistirisk Förening)

Check that spark plug wiring has no fractures.

Inspect the magneto ignition distributor brush and partition segment gaps and that the magneto ventilation holes are open.

Check that the petroflex tubes do not have any grey matter on them. Inspect also the line between the filter and carburettor; change to new when necessary.

Check that the fuel system back pressure valve works correctly.

Remove the oil tank and clean the inside thoroughly.

Remove the outer oil-cooling unit and clean the inside.

Remove both inner oil cooling units and clean the inside.

Clean the inside of the fuel tanks (the fall tank must be removed for this). The main tank drain plug should not be over tightened.

Instruments and gauges

Before every high altitude flight it is necessary to check that there is enough oxygen in the reservoir, the valve is opened, the oxygen line in the cockpit is in good condition and that the maximum oxygen flow is achieved.

Daily inspections

Check the rpm indicators flexible shaft and its couplings.

Wind the clock and adjust to correct time.

Check that there is enough liquid in the compass and that it has free movement.

Check that the compass deviation correction card is clearly placed and firmly secured.

Check that the oil temperature and oil pressure gauges are visibly in good condition.

Check the altimeter and its position.

Check that the tachometer and pitot tube are visibly in good condition.

Check that the main tank fuel gauge works properly and that the wiring is well connected.

Check the oxygen airflow rate.

Check the turn indicator venture tube and that is correctly aligned to the opening. Verify also that the heating works.

Check the brake air pressure gauge and its ducting.

Inspections after every 10 hours of flight

In addition to the daily inspections the oxygen line connectors and valves are checked.

Inspections after every 20 hours of flight

In addition to the daily inspections and inspections after every 10 hours of flight the following procedures and inspections must be done after every 20 hours of flight.

Check the oil pressure and oil heating gauge lines and connections.

Check the fuel pressure gauge lines.

Check the tachometer lines.

Clean the turn indicator suction filter.

Inspect the line between the venture tube and the turn indicator and check that the venture tube is clean.

Check that the compass corrector needles housing is well secured.

Inspections after every 40 hours of flight

In addition to the inspections daily, after every 10 and 20 hours of flight the following procedures and inspections must be done after every 40 hours of flight.

Check the pitch-slope indicator.

Check the fuel pressure gauge lines. Check the compass (that the dampening flanges are not cracked or otherwise damaged, the compass is easily readable, the liquid is clear; the compass base, glass and glass mounting is in good condition).

Test the oxygen equipment and the oxygen mask. Inspect the oxygen lines and connections.

Electrical equipment

Daily inspections

Check that the battery does not leak.

Check the antenna and its mounting.

Check that the electrical wiring and radio wiring connectors are in good condition.

Check the generator mounting and the generator cooling air ducts.

Check the wiring to the generator.

Check the ampere and voltmeter.

Test that the radio remote device works correctly. Run the transmitter and receiver test, to make sure they operate properly.

Swedish Gladiators in flight (Archive Svensk Flyghistirisk Förening)

Test the aircraft navigation light, signal light and cockpit light wiring and pitot tube heating device.
Test the signal light switch.
Test the battery voltage.
Check the radio support brackets.

Inspections after every 10 hours of flight
In addition to the daily inspections.
Measure the liquid level in the battery and its specific weight. Clean the battery from the outside.
Check that the battery support brackets and the surrounding area are not corroded.
Check that the aircraft electrical circuit in whole is in good condition.
Check the insulation between the antenna and ground.

Inspections after every 20 hours of flight
In addition to the daily inspections and inspections after every 10 hours of flight the following procedures and inspections must be done after every 20 hours of flight.

Check that the fuse boxes are clean and intact, and that the fuses and spare fuses are in good condition and of the correct type.

Check that the wiring to the switches, plugs, switch boxes, terminal boxes and fuse boxes are in good condition.

Check that all the switches, plugs, switch boxes, terminal boxes and fuse boxes are clean and in good condition.

Inspections after every 40 hours of flight
In addition to the inspections daily, after every 10 and 20 hours of flight the following procedures and inspections must be done after every 40 hours of flight.

Clean the generator distributor and check that the brush coals move freely.
Check the ampere and volt meter indicators.
Check that the charging current control relay in the cockpit is clean and works properly.
Check that the navigation light covers have maintained their colour and that the covers and threads are intact and clean.

Inspections after every 120 hours of flight

In addition to the inspections daily, after every 10, 20 and 40 hours of flight the following procedures and inspections must be done after every 120 hours of flight.

Check that the generator bearings do not have excess looseness and that the generator distributor is not scratched.

Check that the generator coals are not worn and that the coal springs have the correct tension.

Check the electrical circuit and the radio shielding.

Check the insulation of all wiring.

Inspection instructions

A thorough engine inspection (and repair) is normally done after approx. 200 operating hours

The aircraft interval inspection is done at the same time the engine is removed for its thorough inspection, after approx 200 operating hours. The aircraft is thoroughly inspected and repaired after approx 800 hours of operation.

Right: Latvian Gloster Gladiator No. 123 during taxiing.

Below: Destroyed Russian Gladiators. (Both photos Stratus coll.

Gloster Gladiator Technical Data

Airframe and engine mount

All frame tubing is special alloy steel. The upper and lower spars and the diagonals on the sides are of square tubes and have been attached to each other with straight corner plates. The diagonal tubes are either round or square tubing. The upper and lower spars are of round steel alloy tube. To increase the area where the corner pieces touch the spars, the spars are made to a square profile. The diagonals on the side of the airframe are made of round duralium tubes that are squared at the ends. The airframes crossing tubes are made of round duralium tubes that have rounded end pieces and are further strengthened by bracing wires.

Attached to this basic frame are the fuselage formers, which are made of a lightweight metal. On top if this go the metal stringers, which gives the fuselage its contoured shape. The forward fuselage is covered in aluminium panels, which provided easy access to all the internal parts for the ground crews. The remainder of the fuselage, wings and tailplane are fabric covered. This fabric was attached using Gloster's patented wire-on system. On the side of the fuselage there are fabric covered access hatches that serve as inspection openings for the control mechanism and cables. Immediately in front of the horizontal stabiliser, there are four handles for lifting the tail up. These handles are pocket like crevices in the fuselage covering and shaped for a good grip around the tube. The tail may only be lifted by these handles.

The cockpit has no floor as such. The seat and footboards are bolted onto the framework. The pilot's seat is adjustable by means of a ratchet lever. Operating the lever is similar to operating a cars handbrake. You push in the button and move the lever up or down. Releasing the button locks the lever in position. The MkI has a four-piece instrument panel, while the MkII has a two piece.

Access to the cockpit was by means of a door on either side, which was hinged along the bottom and opened downwards. A door was locked by a lever which when operated engages a metal rod into the sides of the fuselage. The top of the door also acts as the runner for the canopy. The canopy is opened and closed by a hand-operated sprocket and chain.

Remains of a Gladiator Mk II in France 1940. (Stratus coll.)

Destroyed Norwegian Gladiator, 1940. (Stratus coll.)

At the bottom of the fuselage two steel tubes with assemblies to attach the lower wing go through crosswise. These tubes stretch out of the airframe to create the wing root, were the lower wing is attached.

The engine mount was manufactured from steel tube. The engines attachment ring was made of a compressed steel plate. The engine mount is attached to the front of the fuselage with 4 bolts. The front of the fuselage also acts as the firewall. The bottom part of the engine attachment ring is removable, so the engine could be installed and removed without removing the carburettor.

Wings

Both upper and lower wings are separate. The upper wings are attached to a centre section, which is connected to the fuselage by four cabane struts braced diagonally with wires. The lower wings are attached to the wing roots that are built in the fuselage. The wing spars have been made by two roll-formed steel profiles that have been riveted together. The wing spar flanges are 12 cornered tubes that are connected together with corrugated plates. Both the spar flanges and centre plate material is a special steel alloy. The wing ribs have been made from duralium- and steel profiles. The ribs have been put together with rivets. The space between the wing spars is stiffened with wiring. The wing leading edges are strengthened with aluminium plating. In both lower wings there is housing for the landing flares.

On the lower wings, spars 4 and 5 were strengthened to allow fitment of the machine gun and ammunition tank. There are two attachment points for the machine gun. The rear point is adjustable so that the machine gun can be harmonised with the fuselage machine guns.

Undercarriage

The undercarriage units are of a single cantilever design. Each leg consisted of a tubular tapered member with a stub axle. Both members extended up through the fuselage into an A-frame configuration. Dowty internally sprung wheels are fitted along with Dunlop 7" x 19" aerodynamic shaped tyres. The braking system is of the Dunlop air brake type and works as follows. When the brake lever located on the control stick is pressed, air is allowed to go to the distribution valve located at the foot pedals. When the pedals are in the middle position both brakes receive the same amount of air, thus making the braking force the same in both brakes. When the pedals are pressed to the right, the right wheels brake force increases and lessens in the left. The overall braking force is adjusted by the lever in the control stick.

The pressurised air is achieved with a compressor connected to the engine, which constantly maintains pressure in the air tank located behind the pilot. This tank also supplies the air for operating the machine guns. The air system has an oil remover and an air filter to help keep the air clean. Both the oil remover and air filter have to be emptied at regular intervals by removing the bottom plugs. The air pressure in both wheel brakes and air tank can be monitored from gauges in the instrument panel.

The tail wheel assembly is easily removed as a unit and consists of the following main parts: The wheel with its axle and skid shaft with shock absorber and wheel fork. The shocks that come from landings and taxiing, are partly absorbed by the tyre and partly by the shock absorber. When needed to tow or move the aircraft inside a hangar, it is possible to mount a steering spindle on the tail wheel, where there are specially manufactured rollers at the end of that wheel axle for it to attach. Tail wheel type: Either Dunlop AH 5000 or Palmer 637, size 270 x 100 mm.

Elevators and fin

The horizontal stabiliser, elevator, vertical stabiliser and rudder are constructed by riveted steel alloy and duralium sheets. The horizontal stabiliser, which can be adjusted during flight, is constructed in a similar way as the wings having two steel spars and duralium ribs. The horizontal stabiliser halves are attached to the vertical stabiliser and lower air frame spars with tension wires. On the leading spar of the horizontal stabiliser there are brackets for attaching the wiring. The attachment point for the horizontal stabiliser is located between the upper and lower airframe spars. The front spar is attached so it is allowed to move to the transversal support. The rear spar is attached to the bottom part of the horizontal stabiliser adjustment screw, which is pivoted to the support for the airframe upper spars.

The trimming of the horizontal stabiliser is done by a hand wheel located on the left side of the cockpit. The hand wheel has an indicator on it, which indicates the trim angle. Hand wheel movements that might be caused from the stuttering of the aircraft in flight, is prevented by a setting clutch. The hand wheel is connected to the screw shafts chain gear by meanings of cables and chains. The shaft gear, which connects to the adjustment screw is pivoted between two bearing discs, mounted on the screw shaft. When the hand wheel is turned the screw thread moves up or down.

Flight controls

The rudder movement is applied via pedals that can be adjusted lengthwise according to the airframe. The pedal is pivoted by two bearings and has a big lever at the bottom where there are three connecting rods attached. Two of these rods transfer the movement to a cable system located at the sides of the fuselage. The third rod is connected to the brakes air distribution valve. The rudder wiring is made of double woven wire and their end pieces are clamped to the wires. There is no need for splicing the wiring. The elevator and aileron control is done with the control column. The machinegun firing button and brake lever are located on the grip of the control column. The elevator movement is transferred via a push pull rod connected to the lower end of the control column. This rod goes beneath the pilot seat and connects to an idler, right behind the seat. The twin wiring for the elevator are attached to this idler.

Round rods transfer the movement to the ailerons through a chain lever system located at the middle bearing point of the aileron. Where the rods connect at the lower wing and the wing root, steel bridle is used. The lever system has a an axle that is pivoted perpendicular to the wing trailing edge that has a rod attached to the side of the aileron. The aileron levers peg is attached to this le-

Hydraulic flap system. (Drawing from the Gladiator Technical Manual)

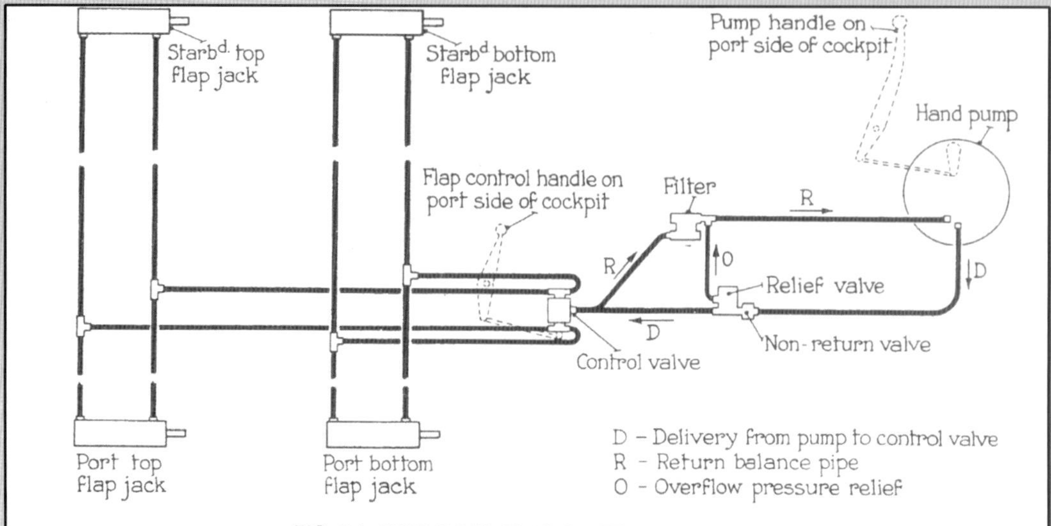

FIG. 54. HYDRAULIC FLAP SYSTEM DIAGRAM

ver. Only the lower wings ailerons get their movement directly from the control column. The upper ailerons are connected via two streamlined tie bars to the lower wings ailerons.

Flaps

On the trailing edge of every wing, at the inner side of the ailerons are the landing/take off flaps. The movement of these is controlled from a pressurised oil system located in the cockpit. The purpose of these is to reduce the aircraft's speed during landing and steepen the glide angle and increase the wing lift. The construction of these flaps is similar to the construction of the ailerons with a steel alloy spar and duralium formers. These are covered in an aluminium skin.

The control unit for the brake flaps is located on the left side of the cockpit. The oil pressure is achieved by a hand pump and is forwarded to the plumbing control valve, which is also on the left side of the cockpit. The plumbing has a pressure relief valve and a backpressure valve. When the flaps are fully extended the pressure relief valve prevents the hydraulic plumbing being damaged if pumping is still continued. The return oil goes through a filter and back to the pump. The flaps are operated by a hydraulic piston connected to a lever system, which operates the brake flap.

The pressure relief valve is adjusted so that it opens when the air pressure rises to an amount that equals approx 95mph. Thus at this given speed the flaps close automatically. Because the flaps will become excessively loaded, they should not be used if this given speed might be exceeded. As mentioned above, the wing lift increases when the flaps are fully opened. It is important that the flaps are not closed during landing, because of the possibility of a stall occurring. During a failed landing it is necessary to first increase throttle and reach a speed of 80mph – 90mph, before closing the flaps. The optimal speed when brakes are fully open is 75mph.

Fuel system

The aircraft has a 63gal main tank and a 20gal gravity tank. During normal circumstances fuel is used from the main tank. The engine driven fuel pump pressurises the fuel via a backpressure valve and fuel filter to the carburettor.

Fuel can be taken from the gravity tank when the lever in the instrument panel is turned to indicate "gravity tank". When the fuel pump works the fuel goes through it and the filter to the carburettor. If the pump for some reason stops working, the fuel flows via the backpressure valve and filter directly to the carburettor. When starting the engine and during preflight running the fuel switch should be normally at the "main tank" position. The gravity tank should be used only in emergencies. The gravity tank should be full before every flight, even if the flight lasts only a short time.

The main tank is located at the front part of the airframe behind the firewall and attached to two brackets. The gravity tank is above the main tank and attached to the upper airframe spars.

Both tanks are manufactured from duralium sheets and assembled with rivets and bolts. The tank filler necks are of large diameter and have quick-release swivel covers. The cover has an attachment point for the ground wire. The main tanks ventilation duct is installed directing aft. The end of the duct on the side of the fuselage, right behind the pilot has a steel strainer. The gravity tank ventilation duct is connected to the main tank.

In addition to the fuel selecting valve (3 way valve), at the gravity tanks bottom there is a shut-off cock at the main tank. This is used when there is a leak between the main tank and 3-way valve stopping a fuel leak to the cockpit. This valve can be used only in an emergency and is normally sealed in the open position.

The main tanks fuel gauge in the instrument panel is electrically operated and powered from the aircraft's electrical system. The gauge has scales to read the fuel level when the aircraft is on the ground and when the aircraft is in level flight. For the fuel gauge to operate it is necessary to press the button immediately on the right side of the gauge. The gravity tanks gauge is of a float type and resides on the left side right in front of the windshield. There is a gauge on the instrument panel that indicates the fuel pressure. This gauge is attached via tubing to the fuel filter. For emptying the main fuel tank it is necessary to loosen the fuel drain lines connection nut 2-3 revolutions. After emptying the main tank the nut must be re-tightened and secured. The gravity tank is emptied by removing the fuel line clamp from the carburettor and turning the selector valve to the gravity tank position.

Lubricating system

The duralium made oil tank is equipped with a quick cycling unit which is located at the top part of the airframe behind the firewall. The tank capacity is 5gal of oil and2 gal of air. There is a filter at the bottom of the tank that keeps the oil free of particles. The oil level is measured with a dipstick located in the tank. The dipstick scale is correct when the aircraft's tail is on the ground. The tank can be emptied by a plug at the bottom of the tank. The oil is led through a feeding line to the engine. This line has a quick emptying unit that allows both the tank and line to be emptied. There is also a ventilation line and an overflow line from the tank to the engine. The return oil is led through an overflow valve to either the oil cooler or directly to the tank. The valve opens and lets the oil flow to the tank when pressure exceeds its limit. The oil goes directly to the tank

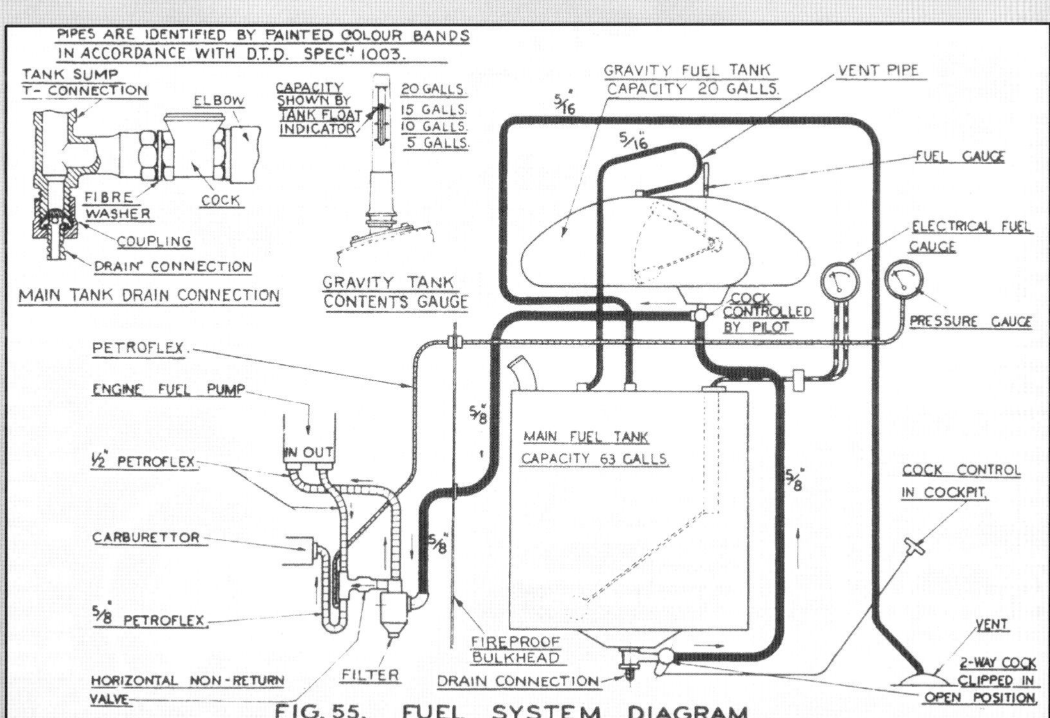

FIG. 55. FUEL SYSTEM DIAGRAM

Fuel system. (Drawing from the Gladiator Technical Manual)

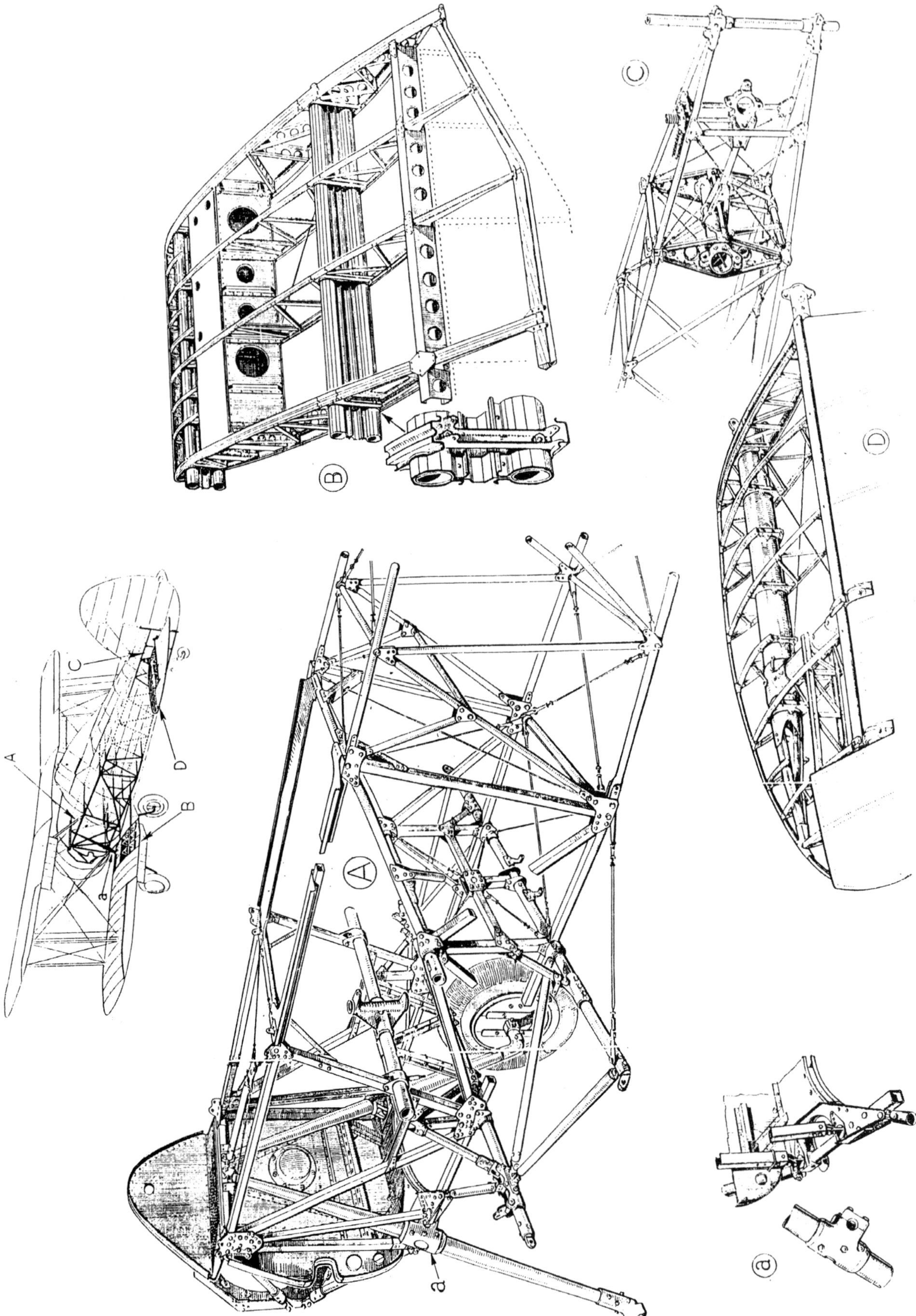

Drawings of the Gladiator, as published in Flight, *1939.*

Line up of the Latvian Gladiators. (Stratus coll.)

only when the three-way selection valve to the oil cooler is closed or when the oil in the cooler is so thick that the overflow valve is opened.

In normal conditions however the oil flows through both inner oil coolers which are located on both sides of the cockpit near the pedal assembly. These coolers also work as the cockpit heaters. After these coolers the oil goes through the three-way valve and depending on the valve position, either directly to the oil tank or to the next cooler, the external cooler. This outer cooler is installed outside of the fuselage on the right hand side, in front of the cockpit.

Before starting a cold engine the selection valve for the oil is turned to “all coolers closed”. The oil flows then in the following method: Oil tank - engine – over flow valve – oil tank. Due to the quick cycling unit only the oil in the filter cup is circulating in the lines. After warming up the oil gets thinner and starts going past the filter mesh. Once the oil in the tank is completely warm, it flows through the previously mentioned openings to the engine. Depending on the outside

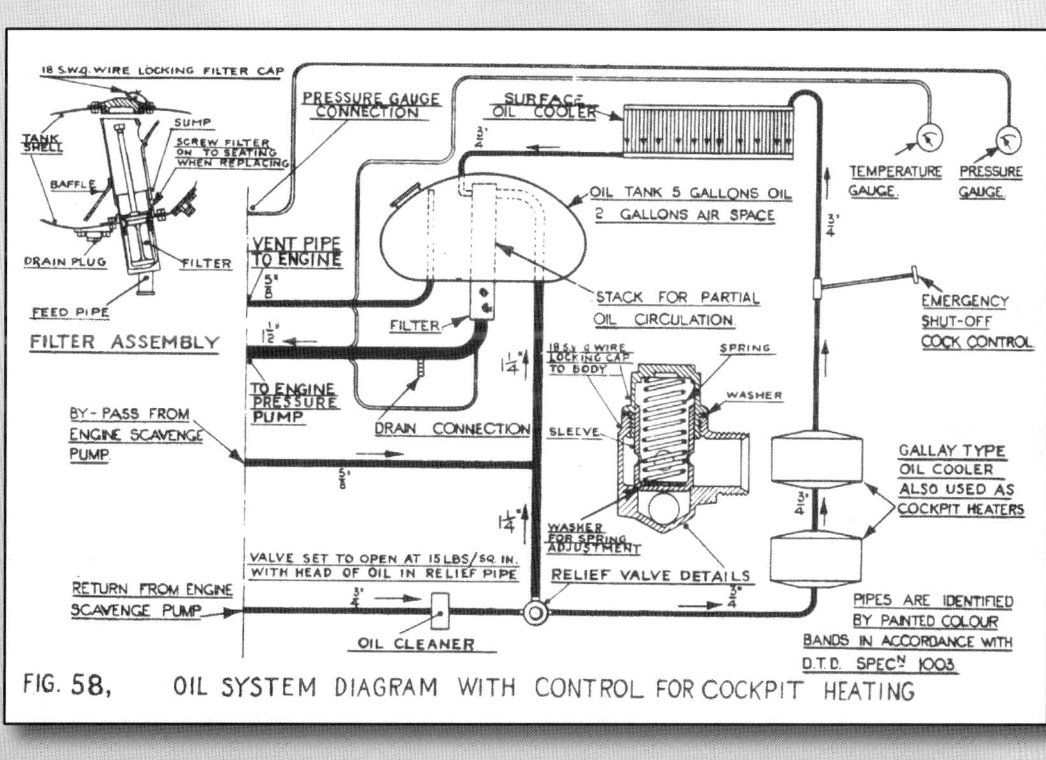

Cockpit heating system. (Drawing from the Gladiator Technical Manual)

temperature either the two inner coolers or in addition also the outside cooler can be selected to be used from the selection valve. When test running the engine, all coolers cannot be simultaneously closed.

The in feed oil temperature can be read from an oil temperature gauge on the instrument panel. The temperature measuring head is installed to the in feed line, near the oil tank. There is no measurement for the return oil in the aircraft. There is a pressure gauge to indicate the oil pressure. This is connected to a line that attaches to the oil pump pressure side. The warm engine start-up lubrication oil is supplied through this same connector.

Engine ignition system

The engine start-up can be done either electrically or by hand crank. The hand crank connects to a toothed clutch, which is on the left side of the aircraft, right in front of the firewall. By turning the crank, the engine crankshaft is slowly rotated through a geared flywheel. Normally the start up is done by an electrical motor that is connected directly to the crankshaft behind the engine. The start-up motor voltage is 24v. The engine start up cannot be done by using the aircraft's own battery, rather a separate ground starting battery should be used. The ground power battery selection switch is located low in front of the firewall. The starter motor is started by pressing the button located in the instrument panel. The starter motor can only be operated in short lengths, to avoid overstressing the motor. The starting magneto is linked via chain to the hand cranks extended axle and starts operating automatically when the starter motor is started. The starting magneto ground connection is established by the starting magneto switch located in the instrument panel. The start up hand crank is stored behind the pilot seat in the cockpit.

Electrical equipment

The electrical components consist of a generator, which charges through the back power relay and the aircraft's battery. The voltmeter indicates the generator's voltage. The ampere meter, +/- 20amp, indicates the batteries charging current and discharging current. From the batteries charging current switch it is possible to adjust the battery charging current to two separate values, by connecting to either the electrical circuit or by separating the resistor. The electrical system supplies power to the radio transmitter (2 units), two machine gun warming devices, three navigation lights, a signal light key, two signal lights, two landing lights, optical sight, fuel gauge, pitot tube heating and four instrument panel lights with their resistance switches.

All fuses for the above equipment, except the radio transmitter fuses are located in the instrument panel. In addition the electrical equipment consists of connection boxes, distribution boxes, coupling boxes and wiring.

Radio equipment

The Gladiator was fitted with a TR9 radio. All aircraft can be equipped with both a receiver and transmitter. The radio is installed on a shelf behind the pilot. The radio control buttons are located on the right side of the cockpit. Here are all the buttons for adjusting the radio, for example transducer button, receiver tuning button and Morse code key. The power for the radio is taken from the aircraft's electrical circuit. The voltage must be 12v. The current usage when receiving is about 3amp and when sending 12amp. There are some transformers under the radio, which change the aircraft's electrical circuit current to suit the radio. All aircraft components are electrically tied together. The fixed radio antenna is strung between the horizontal stabiliser and wing fittings and the antenna mast located behind the cockpit. The antenna mast is used also as the antenna wire infeed location.

Landing flare equipment

On both lower wings just outboard of the wing struts there is a housing, which holds a Frazer-Nash type landing flare. The flare, when not in use is sealed in to its housing. The flare is released from the cockpit via an electro magnet. This electro magnet releases the housing door. As the door opens a spring forces the flare holder out into the slipstream and at the same time the flare is ignited.

Armament

Initially the Gladiator was fitted with two Vickers MkV machine guns in the fuselage and either two Lewis (K6129-K6151, K7892-K7928) or Vickers (K7929-K7938) machine guns under the wings in a streamlined blister. The fuselage guns fired through the propeller by means of an interrupter gear, while the wing guns fired outside the propeller arc. Ammunition capacity was 600 rounds for the fuselage guns and a 97 (Lewis) or 100 (Vickers) round drum for the wing guns. Later Gladiators were fitted with Browning machine guns in the fuselage and wings; these wing guns now held 400 rounds of ammunition.

The spent cases and links were retained in a large tank in the fuselage. This tank was removed through an access hatch in the bottom of the fuselage. The spent cases and links of the wing guns were ejected overboard.

Machine gun firing system

Both fuselage and wing machinegun are operated using pressurised air from the wheel brake system air supply tank. An airline has been drawn from the four-way valve of the braking system to the trigger on the flight stick. When the trigger is pressed the valve opens letting air go to the 7 way valve located at the underside of the right foot pedal. From this valve two lines go to the wing machine gun firing cylinders and two go to the fuselage machinegun synchroniser cylinders. When pressing the trigger on the control column all machineguns operate at the same time.

Specification

	Gladiator Mark I	Gladiator Mark II	Sea Gladiator
Engine	Mercury IX	Mercury VIIIA/AS	Mercury VIIIA/AS
Wing span	32ft 3in	32ft 3in	32ft 3in
Length	27ft 5in	27ft 5in	27ft 5in
Height	10ft 4in	10ft 4in	10ft 4in
Weight	3,216lb	3,444lb	3,553lb
Top speed (sea level)	210 mph	215 mph	210 mph
Top speed (5,000ft)	226 mph	224 mph	220 mph
Top speed (10,000ft)	245 mph	249 mph	245 mph
Top speed (14,500ft)	253 mph	257 mph	253 mph
Top speed (17,500ft)	250 mph	253 mph	248 mph
Top speed (20,000ft)	236 mph	239 mph	230 mph
Take-off run	125 yards	125 yards	130 yards
Take-off to 50ft	200 yards	180 yards	205 yards
Landing run from 50ft	240 yards	250 yards	260 yards
Stalling speed	53 mph	54 mph	55 mph
Range	352 miles	444 miles	320 miles
Endurance	1hr 36mins	2hrs 6mins	1hr 20mins
Fuel load	83 gallons	83 gallons	83 gallons

Scale plans

Gloster Gladiator Mk I.
1/72 scale plans.

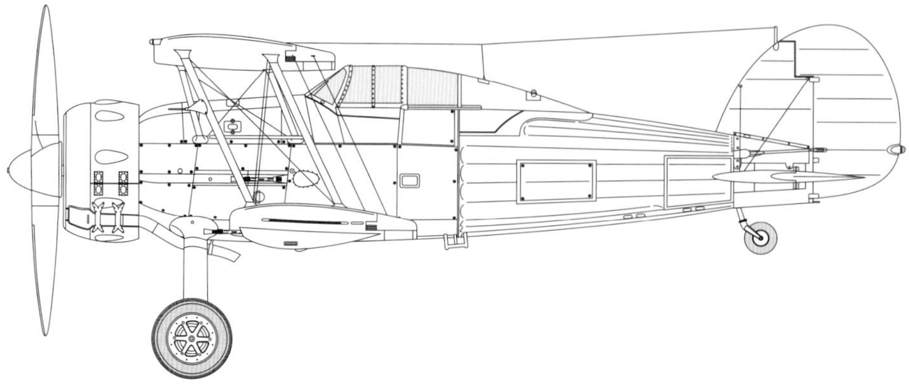

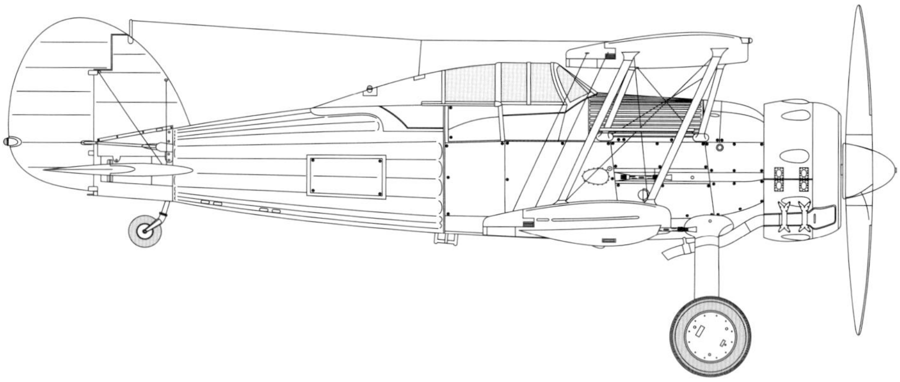

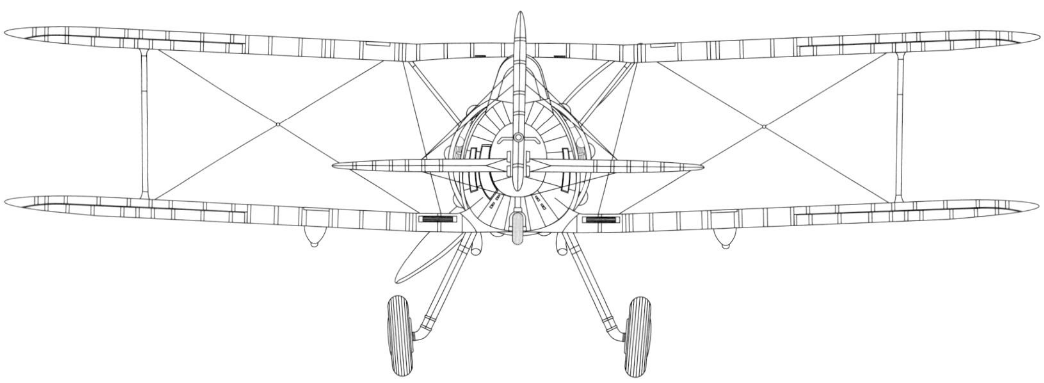

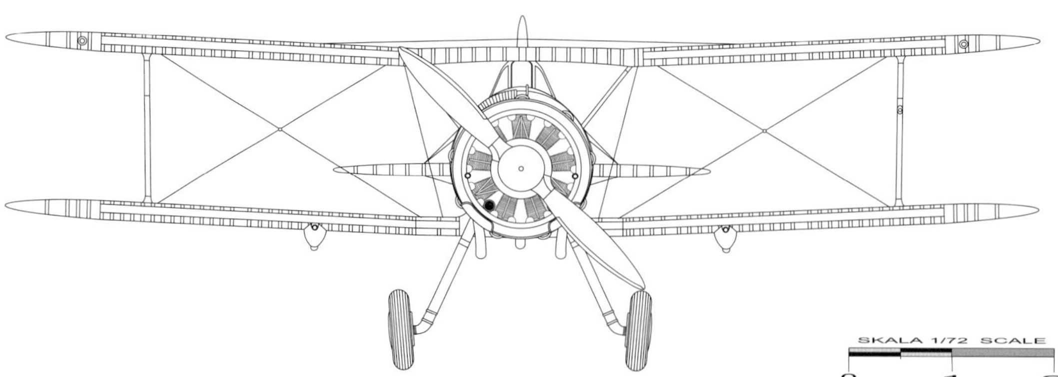

Gloster Gladiator Mk I.
1/72 scale plans.

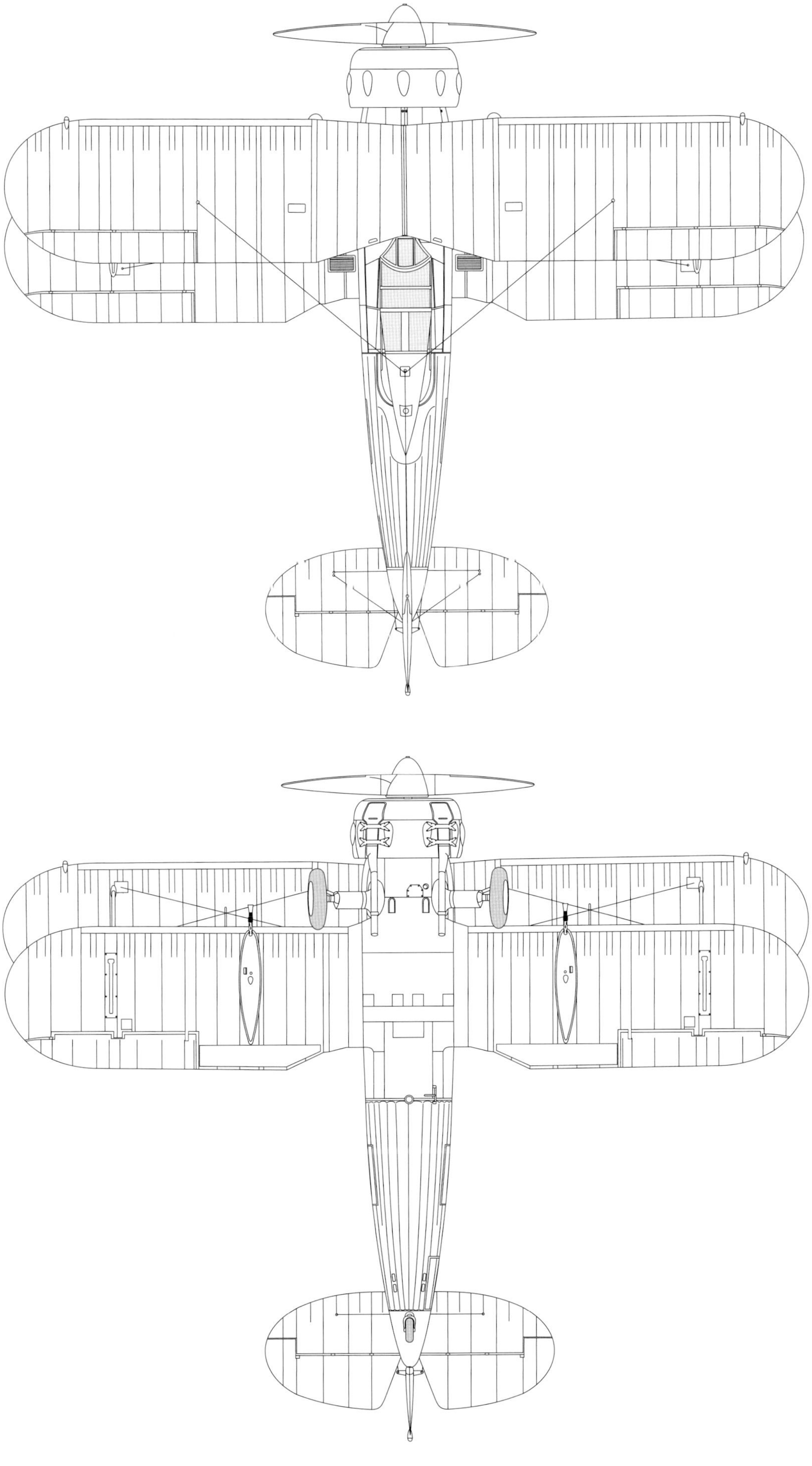

SS 37 prototype.
1/72 scale plan.

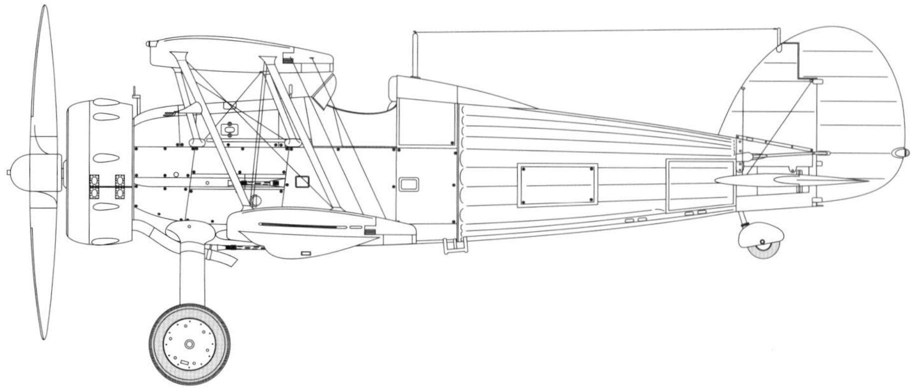

Finish Gladiator with skis.
1/72 scale plan.

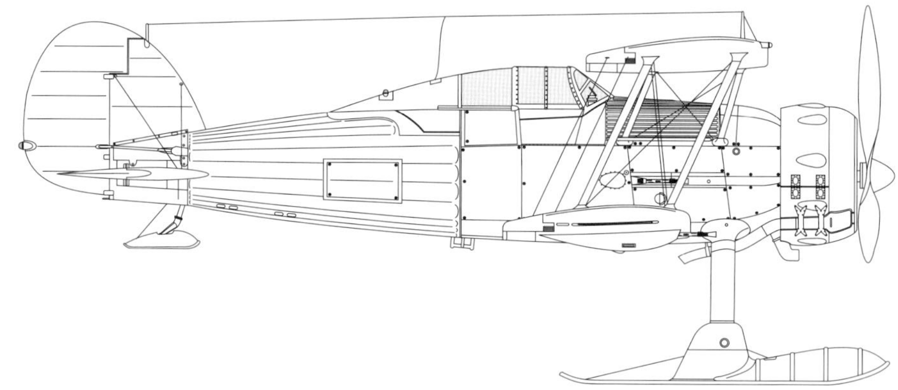

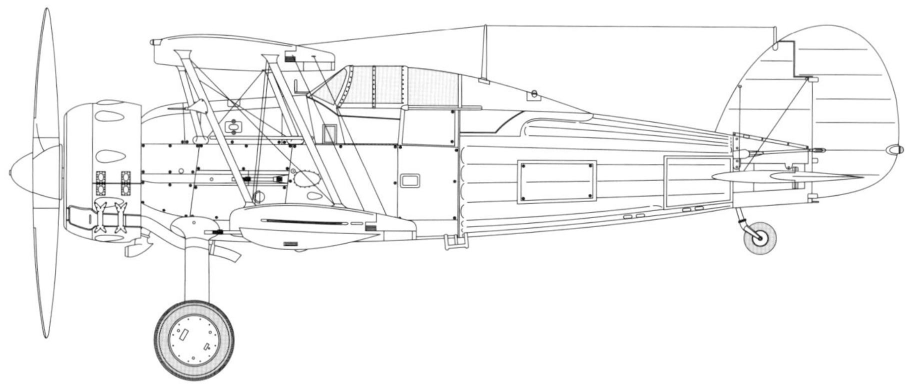

Swedish Gladiator - J8.
1/72 scale plan.

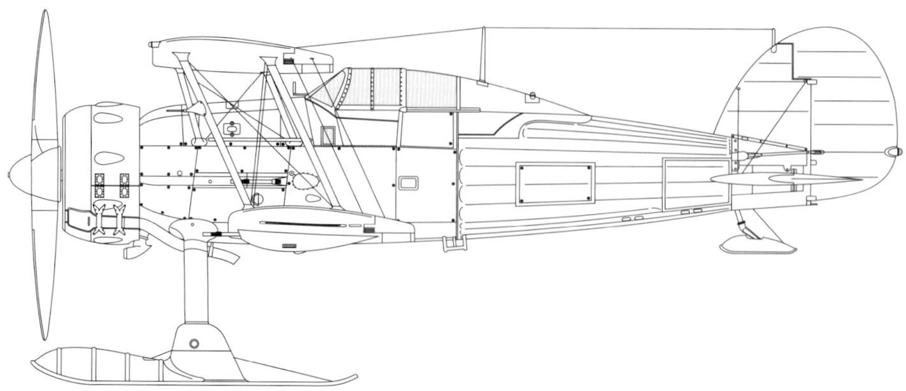

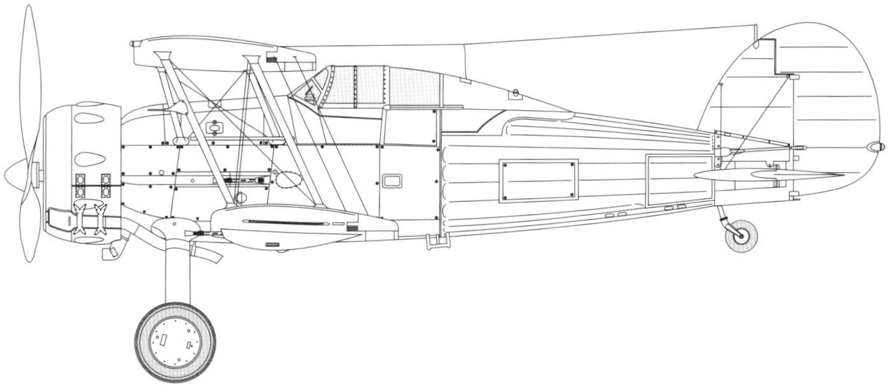

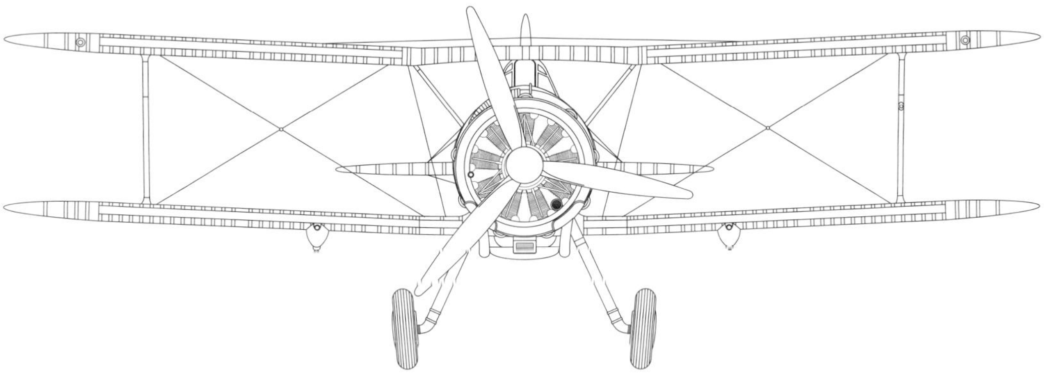

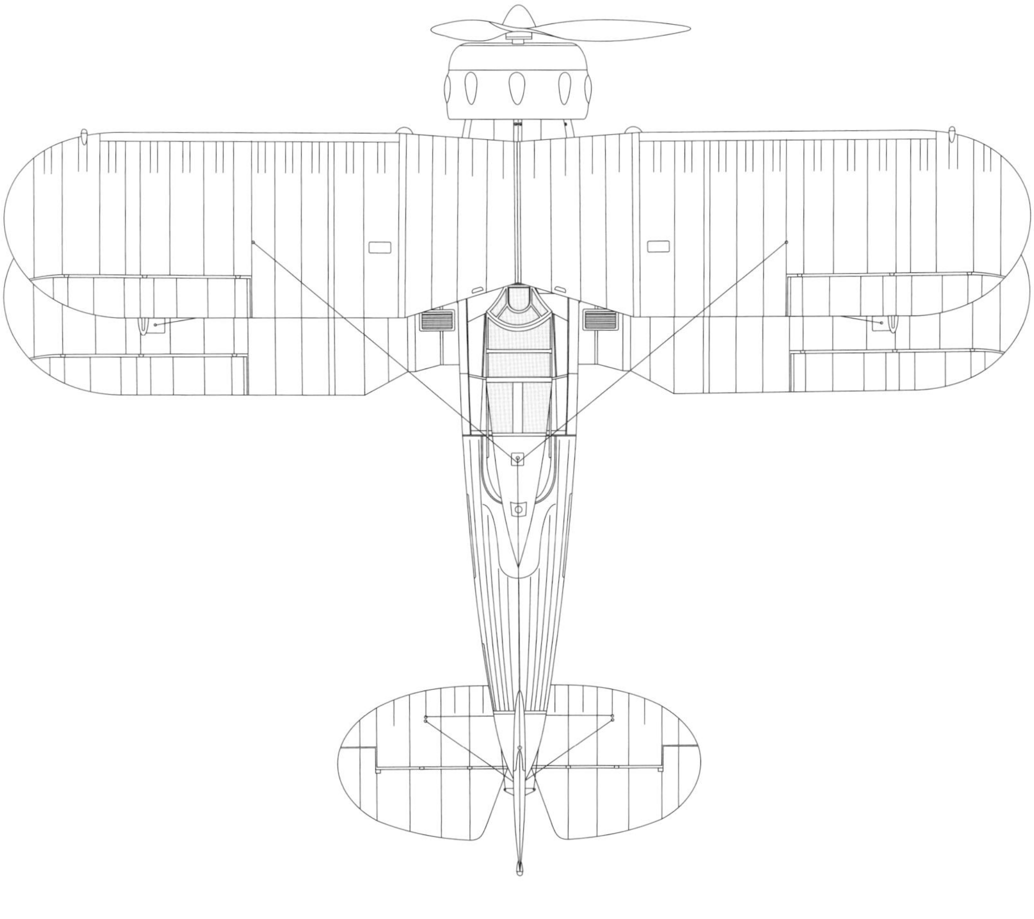

Gloster Gladiator Mk II.
1/72 scale plan.

Gloster Gladiator Mk II - Met Flight version. 5” dia. lamp - to illuminate strut thermometres, below the side windscreen. 1/72 scale plan.

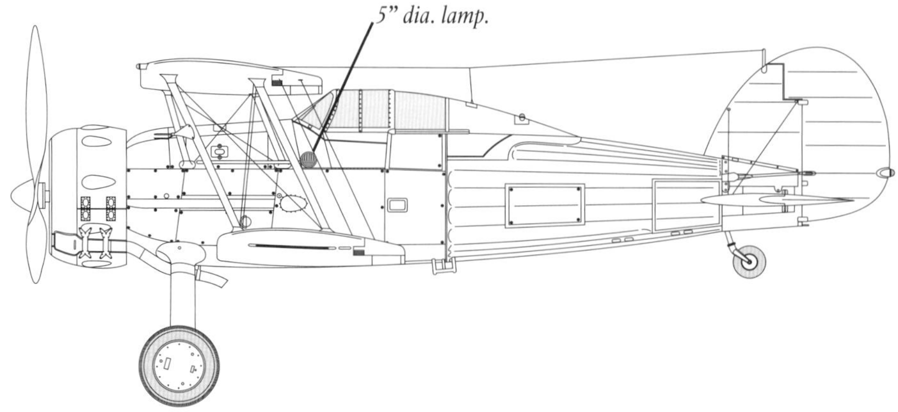

Norwegian Gladiator with skis. 1/72 scale plan.

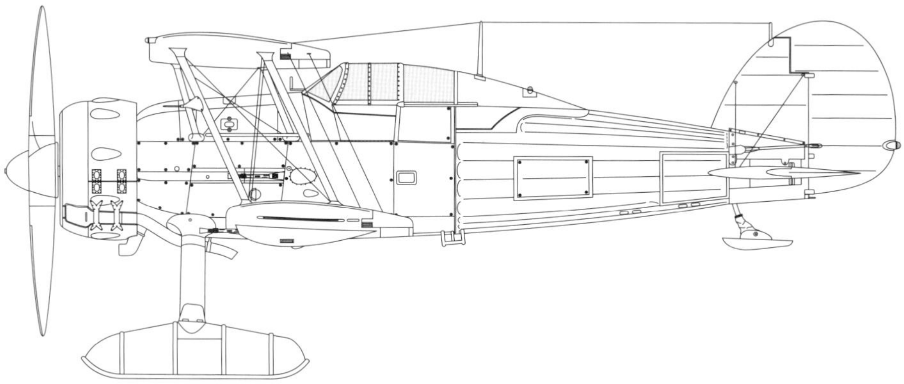

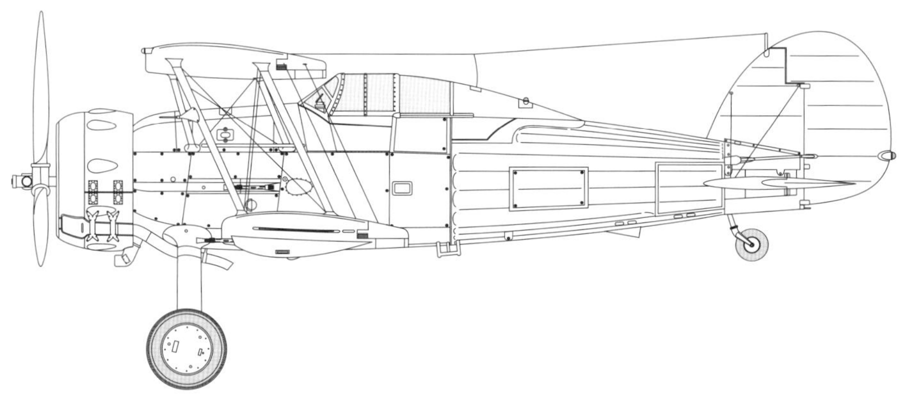

Gloster Sea Gladiator converted at Malta. 1/72 scale plan.

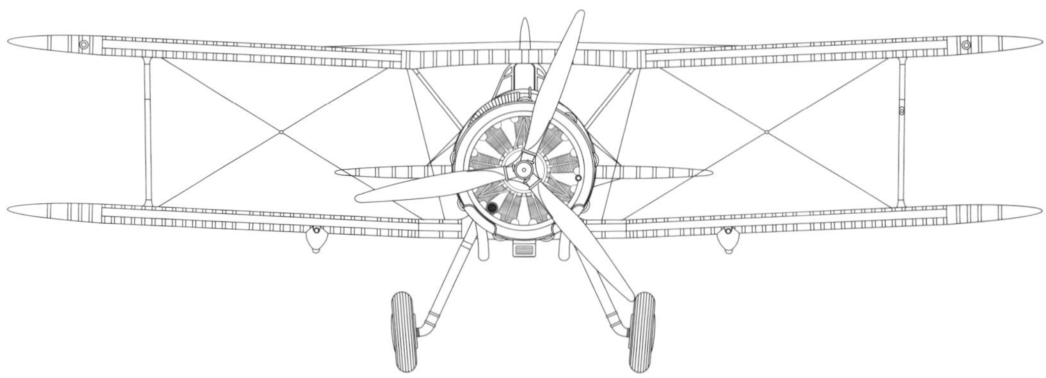

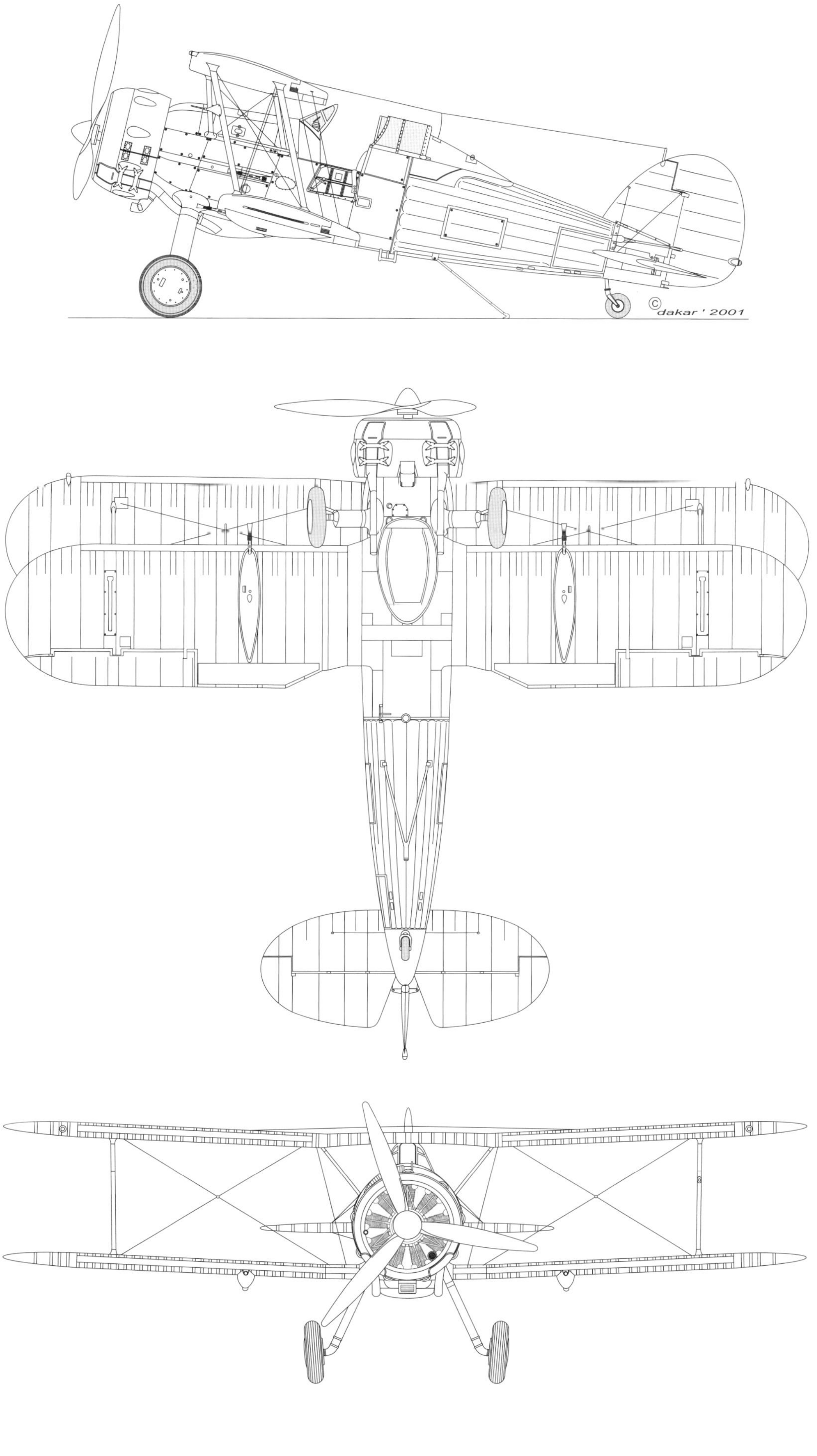

Gloster Sea Gladiator.
1/72 scale plan.

(M. Ryś)

(M. Ryś)

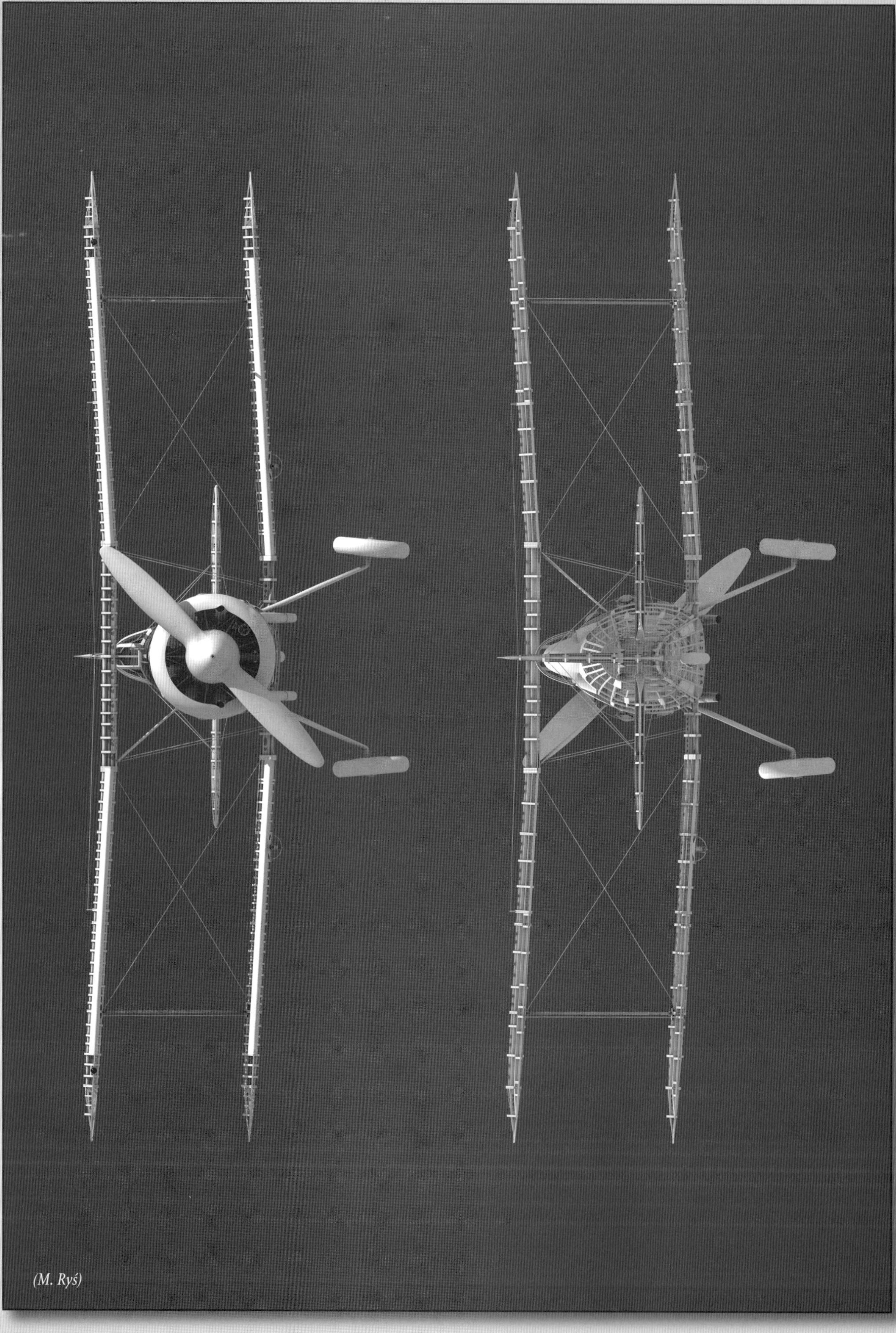

(M. Ryś)

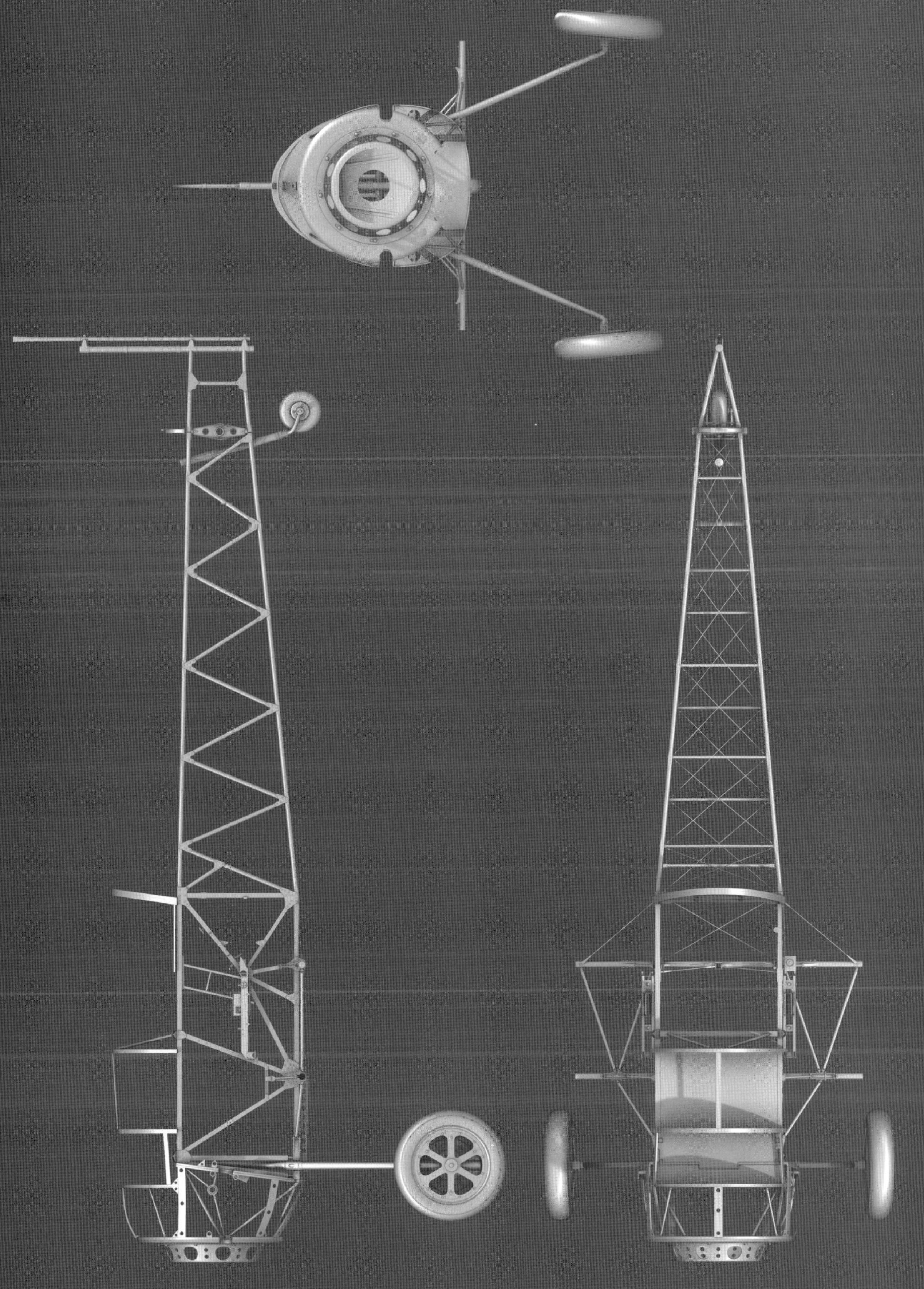
(M. Ryś)

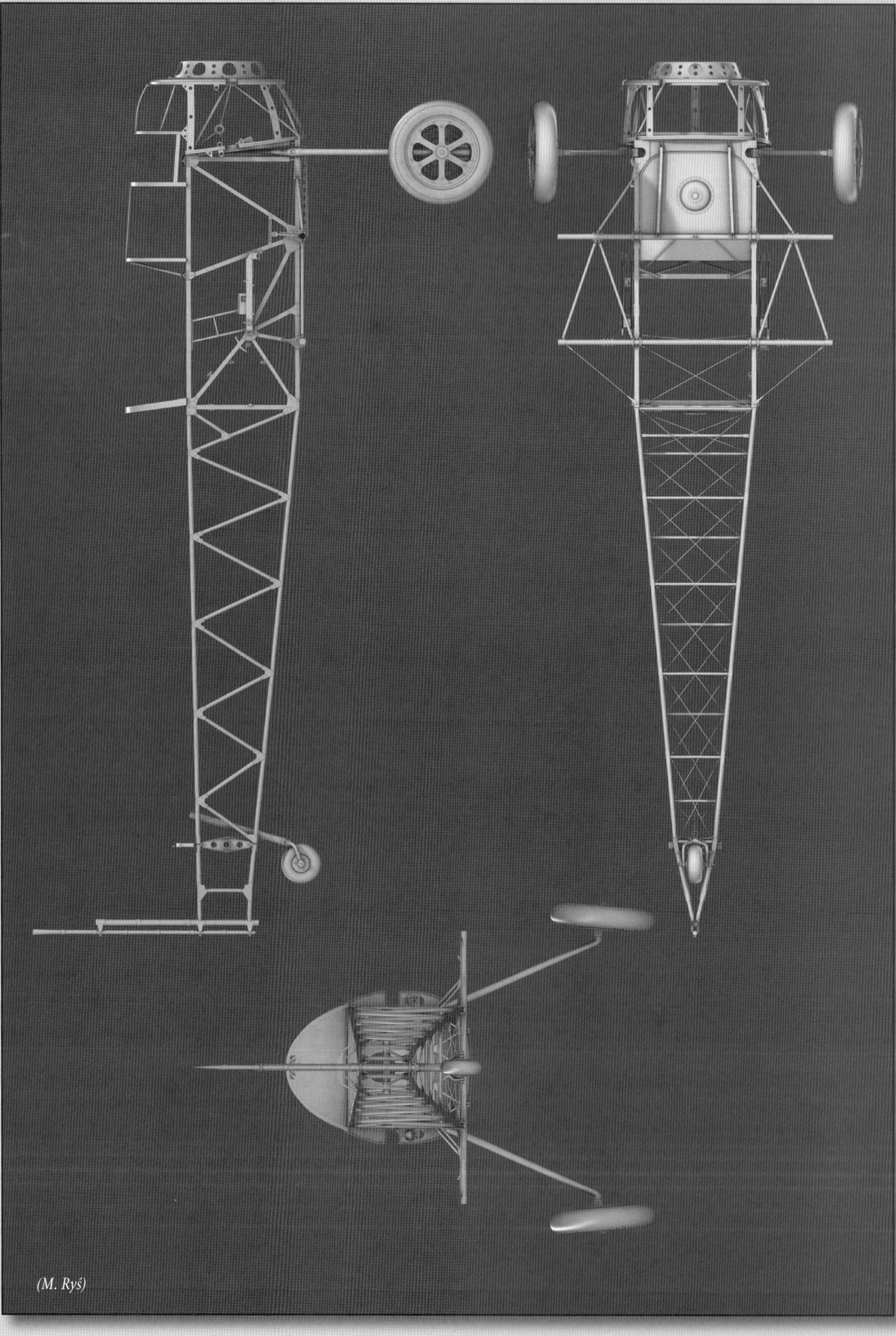

(M. Ryś)

Gladiator in Detail

(M. Ryś)

Two shots of Gladiator Mk I G-AMRK of the Shuttleworth Collection showing the classic biplane design of the late 1930s. (A. Juszczak)

Above: 3D drawing showing Gladiator construction. (M. Ryś)

Below: The Dzus fastened quick-access side-access panels removed. (R. Pęczkowski)

Fuselage construction. (M. Ryś)

Fuselage construction. (M. Ryś)

Another view of the Gladiator with the side-access panels removed. (R. Pęczkowski)

Bottom: *The The Fighter Collection's Gladiator's fuselage after restoration awaiting wings. (A. Juszczak)*

Above: *Rear part of the fuselage just after the canopy. Note the shape of the ply fairing for the canopy and pilot's headrest. (R. Pęczkowski)*

Left: *Three photos of the forward part of the fuselage with access panels removed. (R. Pęczkowski)*

Below: *Details of the oil cooler mounted on top of the fuselage. (R. Pęczkowski)*

***Above:** Top part of the fuselage in front of the cockpit. The fuselage strut fairing is visible. (R. Pęczkowski)*

***Above, right:** Details shot of the formation light mounted on the ply fairing behind the cockpit. (R. Pęczkowski)*

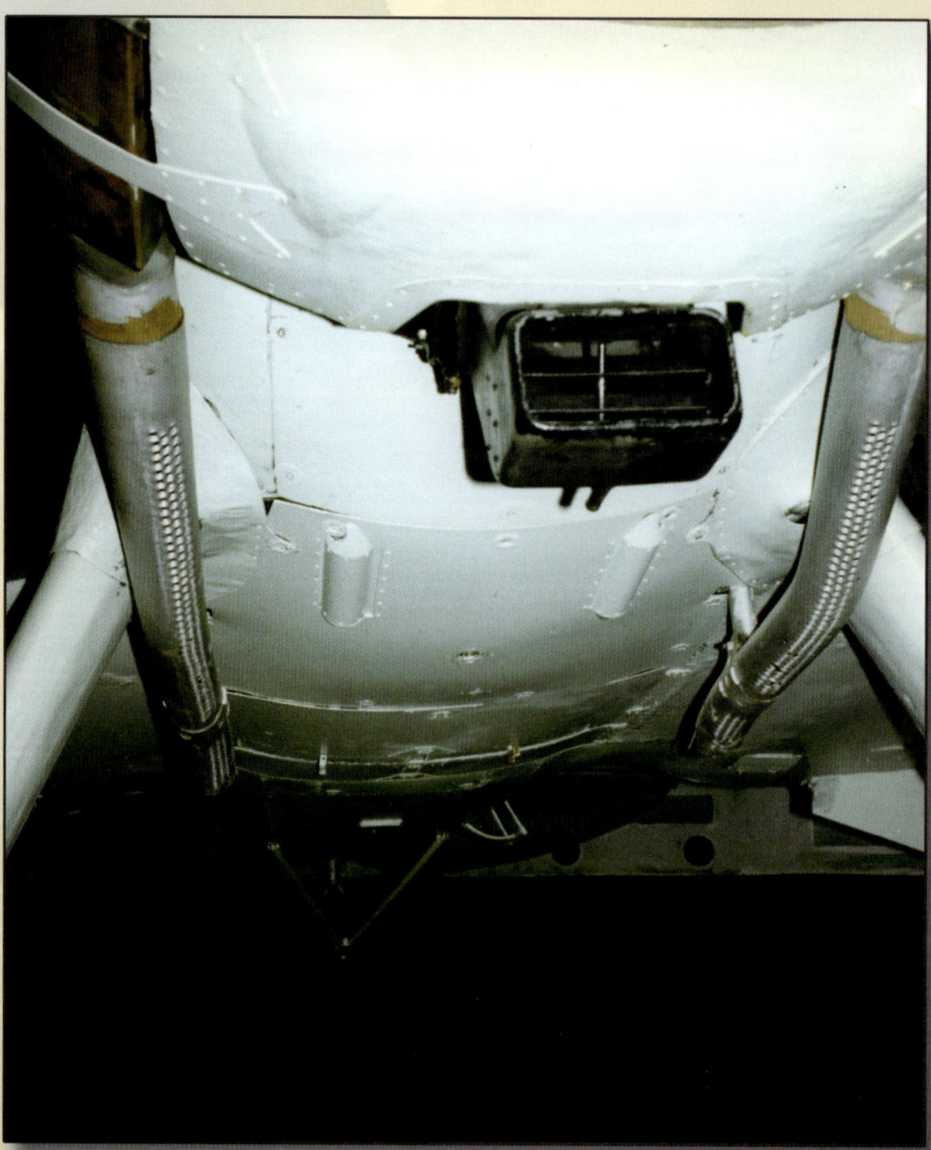

***Right:** The underside of the fuselage of Gladiator N5903 when mocked up as a Sea Gladiator at the Fleet Air Arm Museum, with the carburettor air intake in the foreground. The mock-up arrestor hook is also visible in the rear. (R. Pęczkowski)*

***Bottom, right.** Formation light from the right. (R. Pęczkowski)*

Top & above, left: *Starboard side of the fuselage. The fuselage construction is visible. (A. Juszczak)*

Above: *'Lift Here' marked hand-holes are visible. (R. Pęczkowski)*

Left: *Details of the pilot's access step. (R. Pęczkowski)*

Rear part of the fuselage, starboard side.
(All photos R. Pęczkowski)

Left: *Compressed air valve.*

Below, left: *Inner side of the starboard side removable panel, over the gun breech.*

Below: *The inside of the fuselage. Notice the Warren girder style tube construction of the fuselage with wooden formers and stringers over it to create the stramlined shape.*

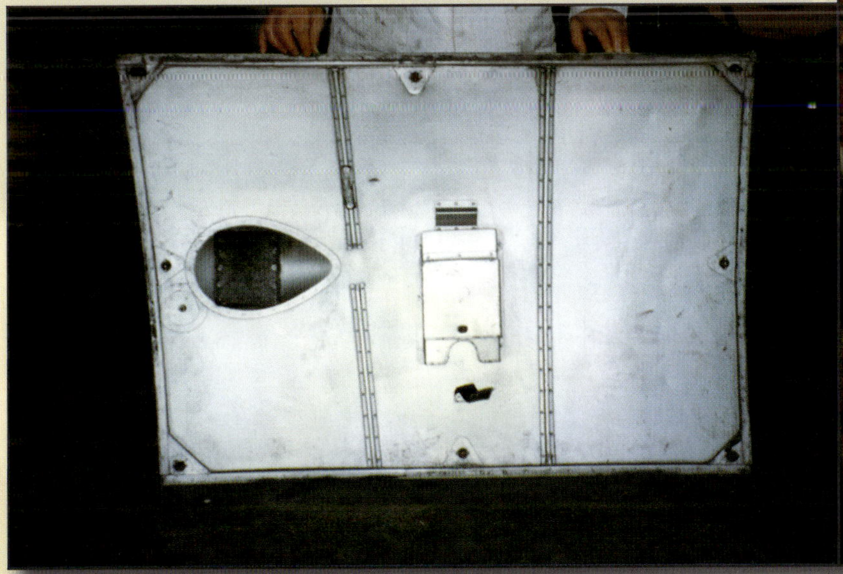

The starboard side of the Gladiator at the RAF Museum, Hendon.
(All photos R. Pęczkowski)

Details of the fuselage construction, with the control cables visible.
(All photos R. Pęczkowski)

Left: *The compressed air bottles for the brake system, with greater detail of the Warren truss construction. (A. Juszczak)*

Below: *The Fighter Collection's Gladiator under restoration. (R. Pęczkowski)*

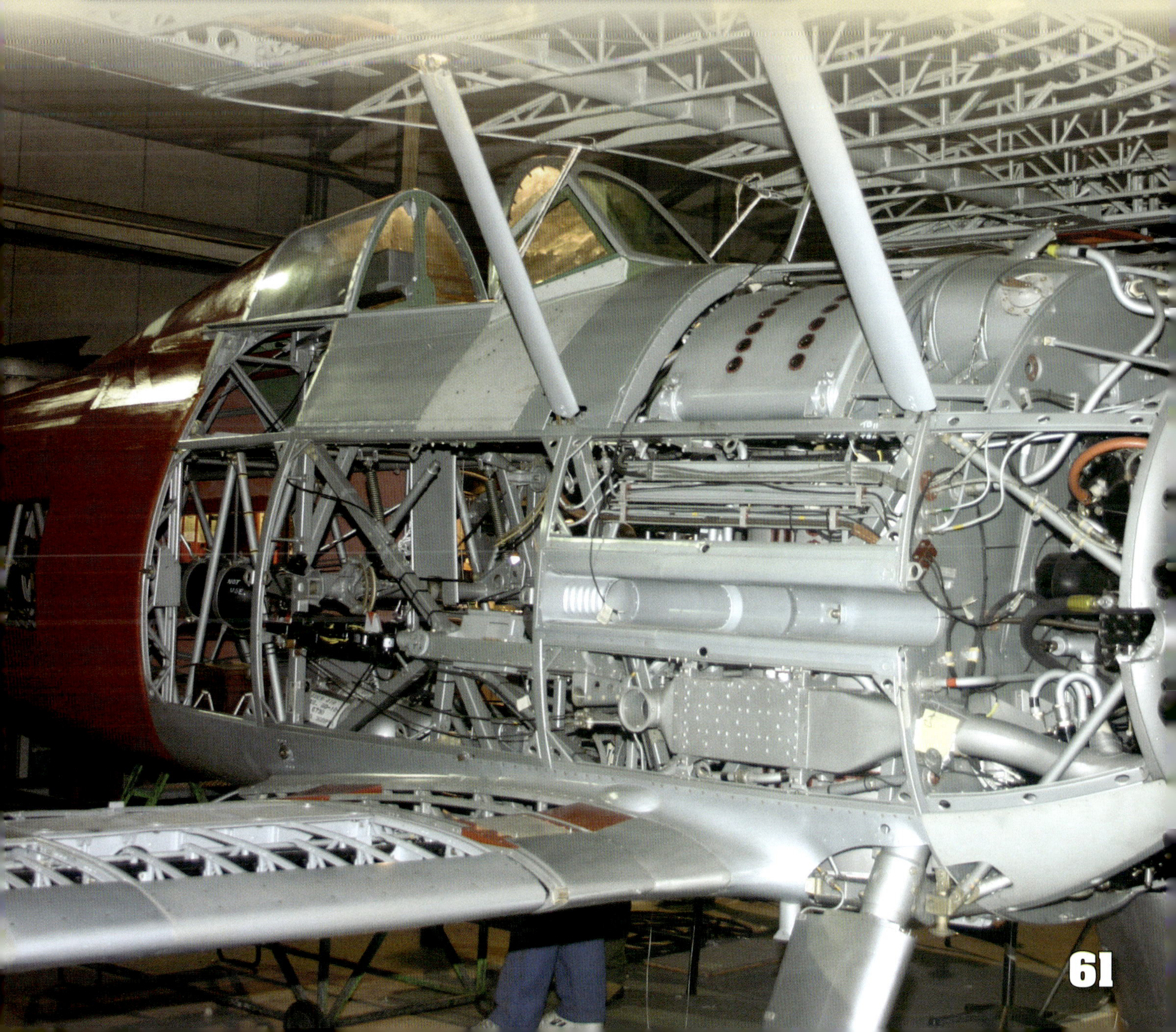

Top: 3D drawing showing wing construction. (M. Ryś)
Shuttleworth's Gladiator in flight. The wing planform is well visible. (J. Kightly)

Underside of the lower wing. The wing machine gun has been removed.
(All photos R. Pęczkowski)

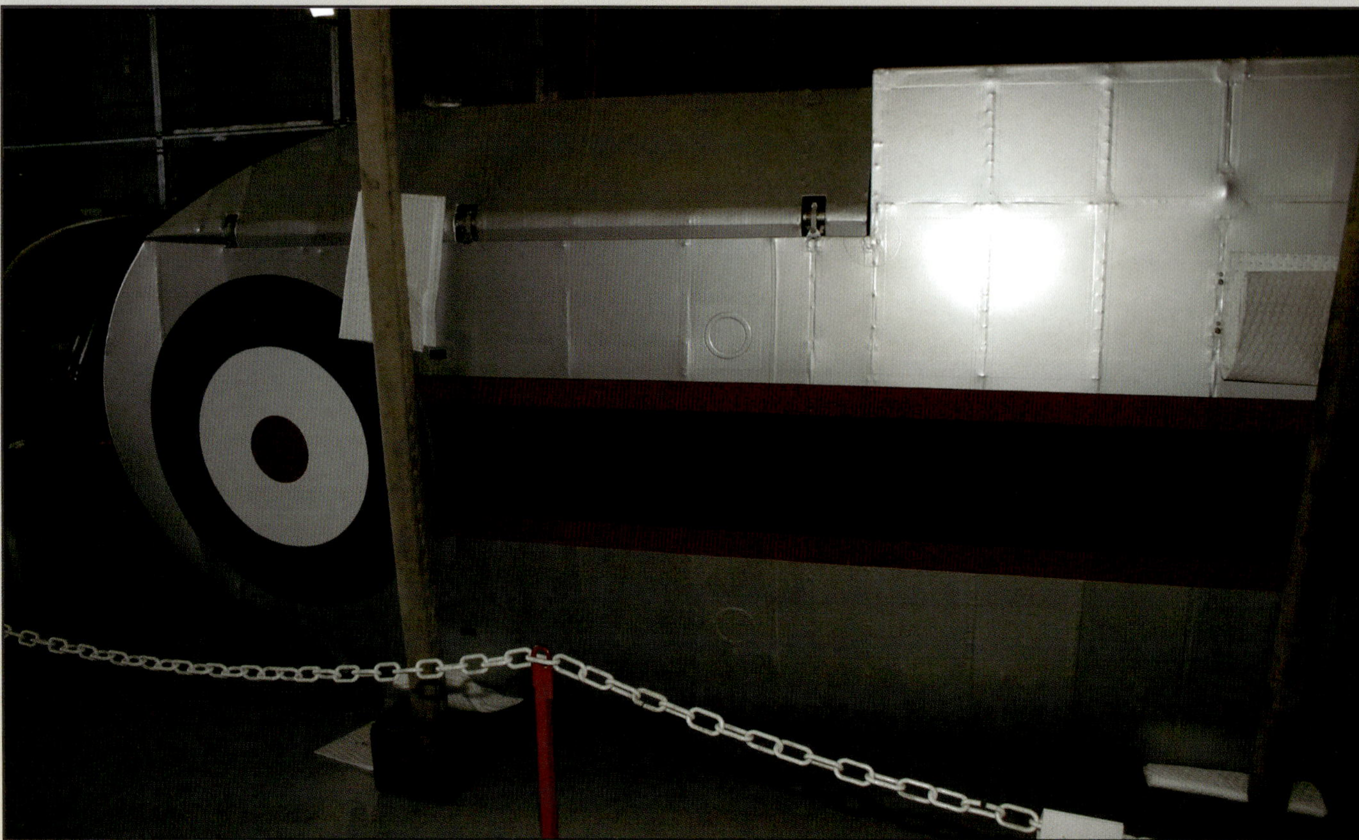

65/81275
CX
W/T

Opposite page: Photos showing top side of the upper wing. (R. Pęczkowski & A. Juszczak)

This page.

Top: Upper centre section construction. The spars and ribs are clearly visible, as is the slight 'Vee' in the leading edge. (J. Kightly)

Middle: The wing skinning of the upper wing, also showing the wing to centre section join. (R. Pęczkowski)

Bottom: Starboard upper wing tip and aileron. (R. Pęczkowski)

The underside of the starboard upper wing. The interplane struts and cross bracing are visible, and note the aileron control cables.

Centre struts and bracing. Note how the bracing joins the wing.

Top side of the wings. The wing handholds are also visible. (All photos R. Pęczkowski)

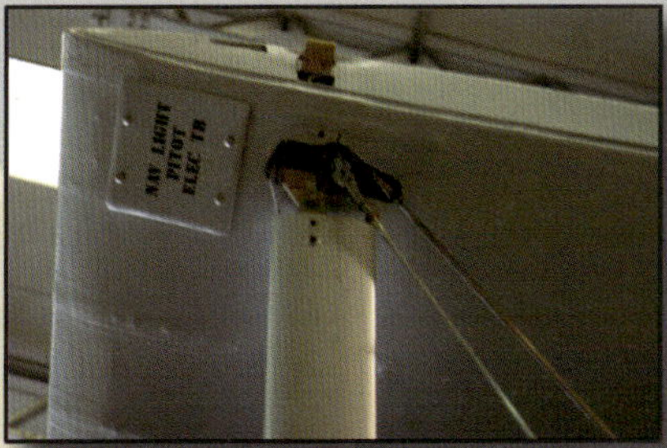

Above: Details of the centre-section struts and bracing. (R. Pęczkowski)

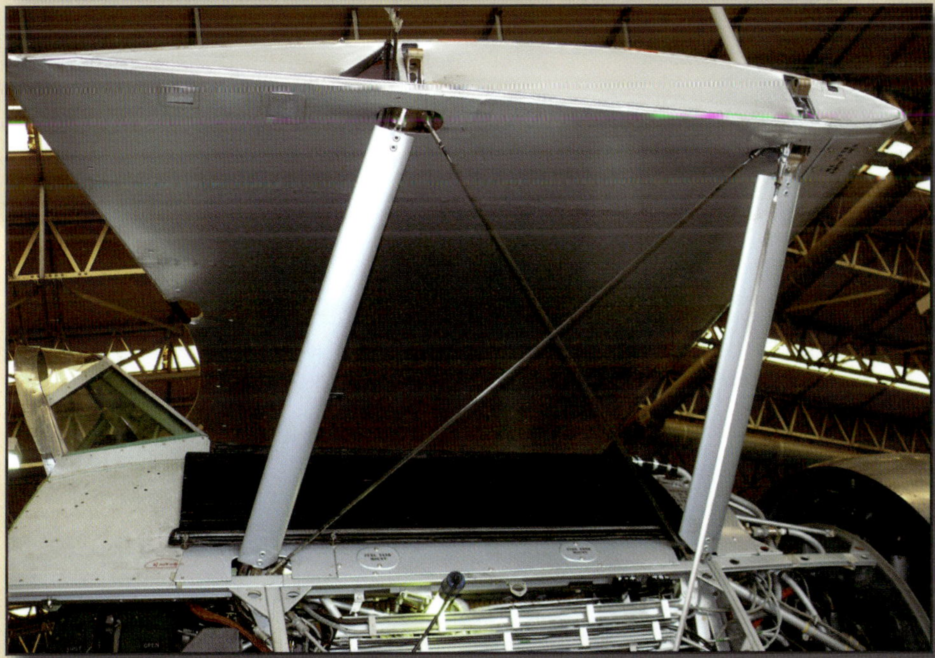

Left: Wing centre-section details. Outer wing mounts are also visible. (A. Juszczak)

The upper starboard wingtip, underside, showing the navigation lamp. (R. Pęczkowski)

Right: Corrugated rubberised non-slip footstep, port wing.

Below: Details of the bracing mounting.

Bottom: *Upper part of the port, lower wing. Details of the struts and bracing are visible.*
(All photos R. Pęczkowski)

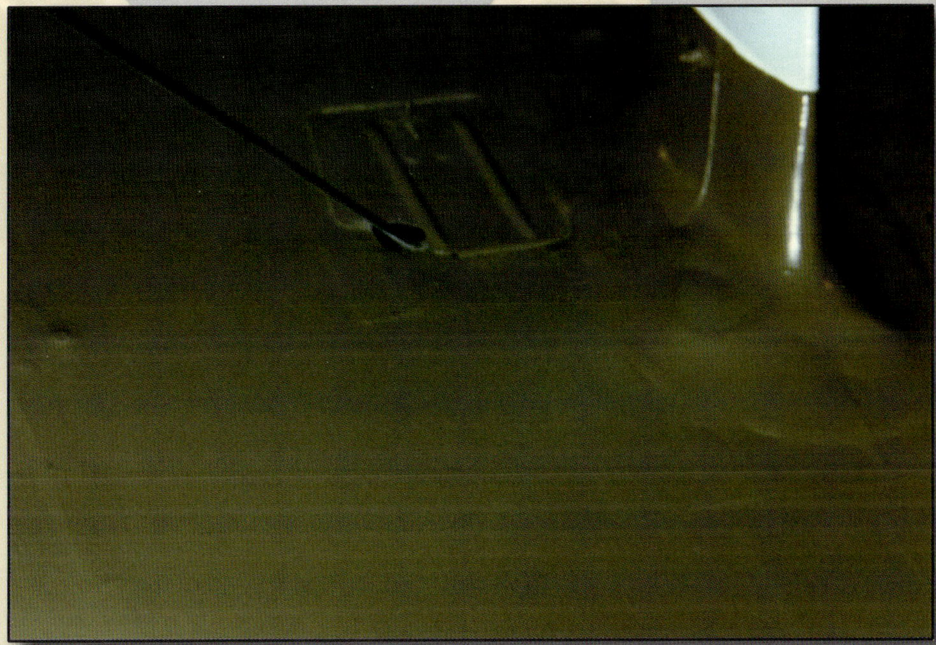

Above: Starboard, lower wing.

Left: Outer strut fairing and bracing mount, also showing the access. (Both photos R. Pęczkowski)

Port, lower wing, with the aileron control cables visible. (M. Bronkowski)

Port, upper wing, handhold details. (A. Juszczak)

Top: Shuttleworth's Gloster Gladiator at touchdown with the flaps in landing position. (A. Juszczak)

Right: The upper wing flap in the landing position, with the construction details visible. (R. Pęczkowski)

Right: Lower, port flap in landing position. (A. Bronkowski)

Below: The flap position indicator. (R. Pęczkowski)

Two 3D drawings showing wing and tail construction. (M. Ryś)

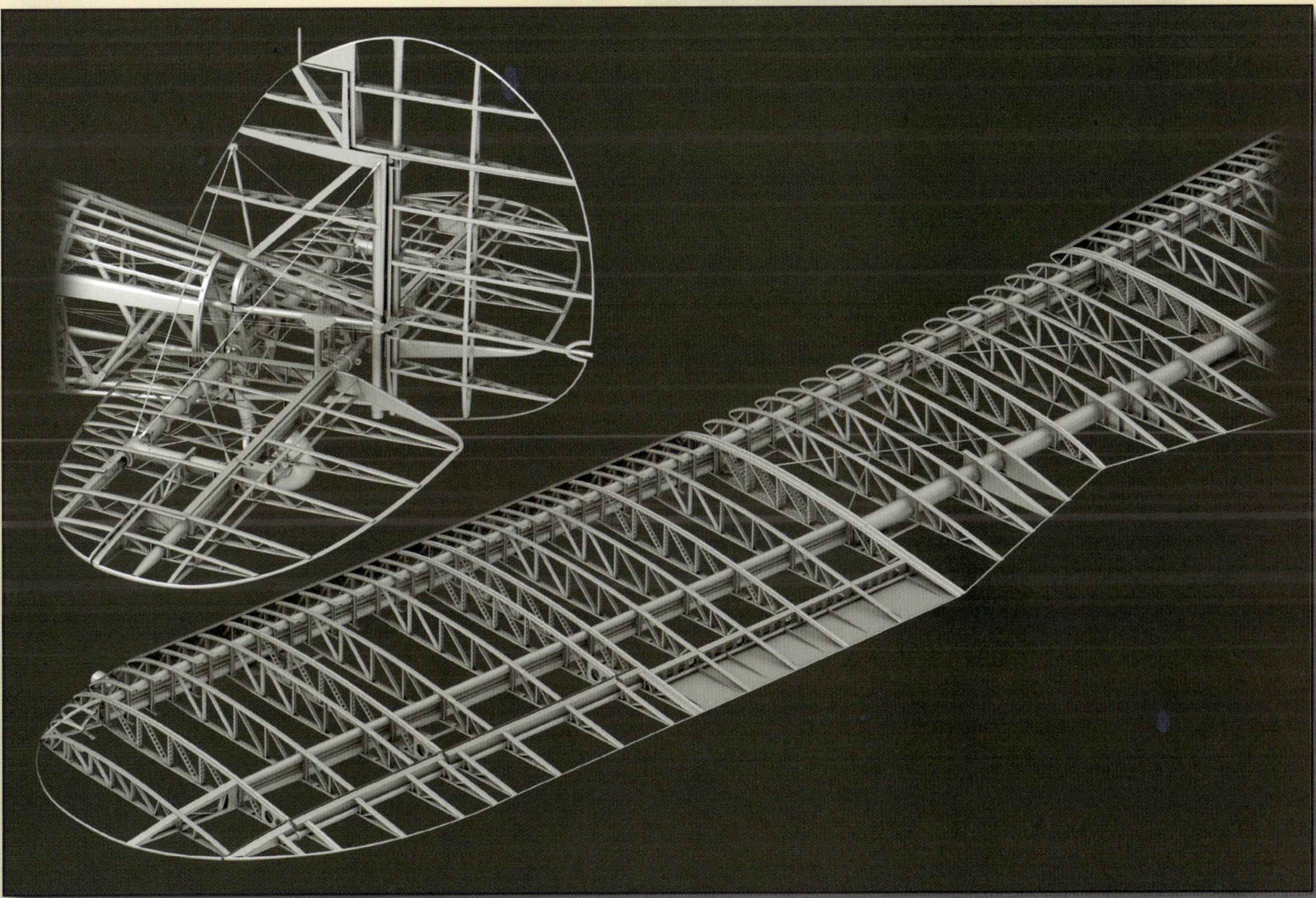

The Gladiator's canopy in the closed position, side view. (R. Pęczkowski)

The fixed rear cockpit canopy, in moulded Perspex. (R. Pęczkowski)

Bottom, right: The windscreen frame, seen from the rear, with the gunsight visible. (A. Juszczak)

Bottom, left: Side view of the windscreen. (R. Pęczkowski)

The sliding part of the canopy. This could be left open in flight, or jettisoned in an emergency. (R. Pęczkowski)

***Bottom:** The fixed windscreen and the rear fixed glazing are visible, and the pilot's side access door is lowered. (A. Juszczak)*

Next pages.
***Left page:** 3D drawing of the Gladiator cockpit. The gunsight is not shown for clarity. (M. Ryś)*

***Right page:** The Fighter Collection's Gladiator cockpit during restoration. Note that some components are yet to be fitted. (A. Juszczak)*

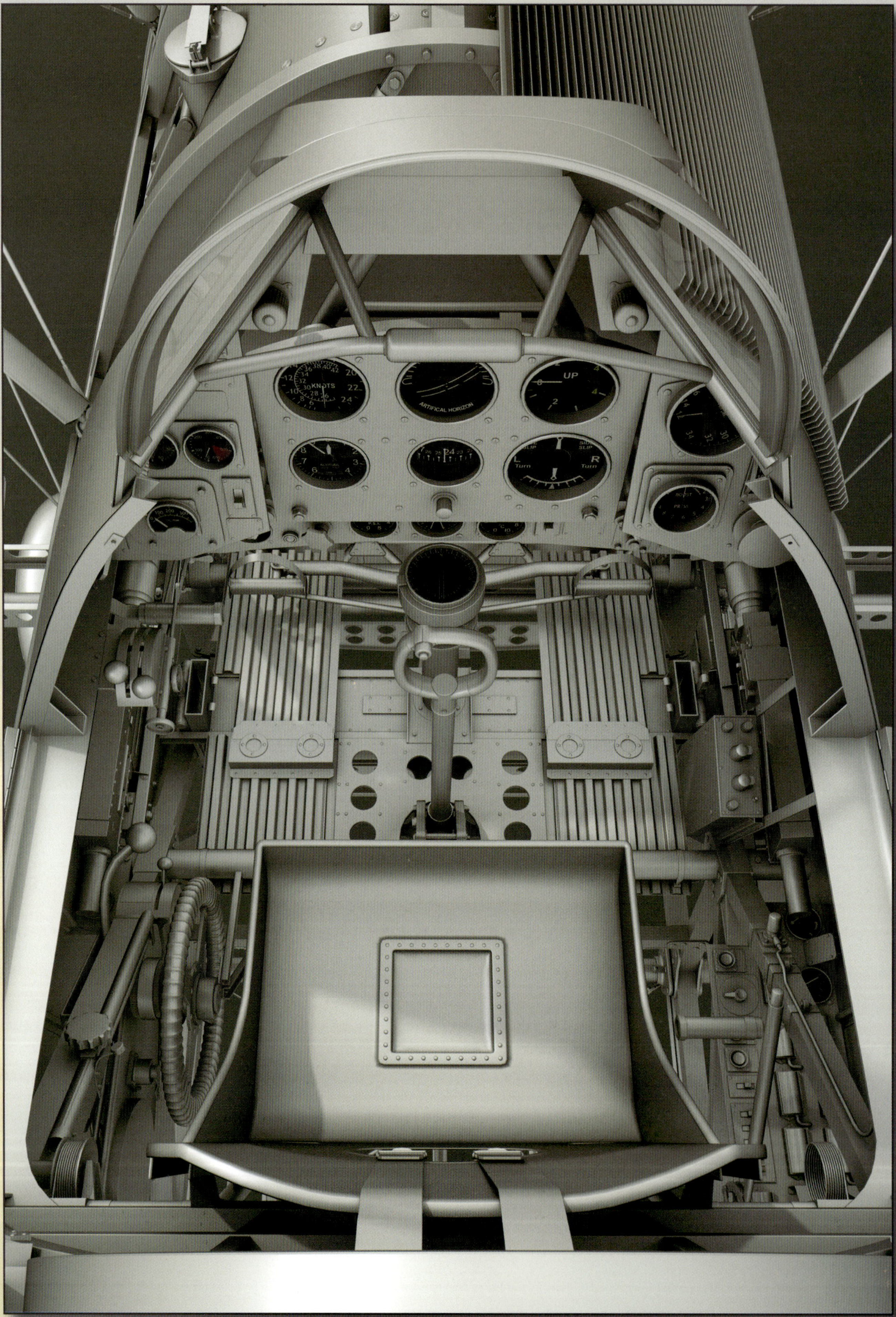
KNOTS
ARTIFICAL HORIZON
UP
L
R
Turn
Turn

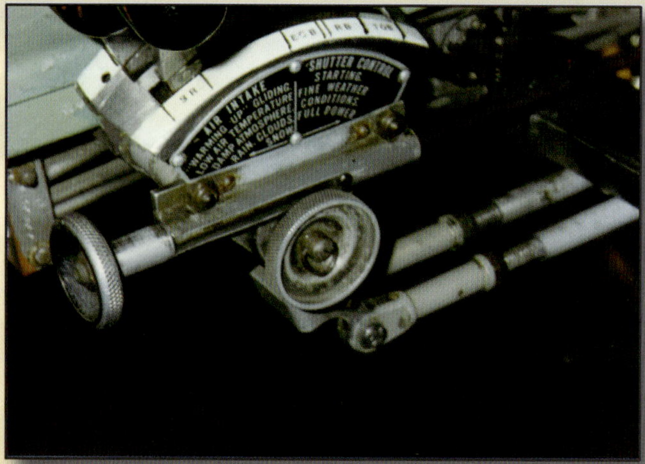

Top: The instrument panel of the Gladiator, with the gunsight mount visible. (R. Pęczkowski)

Above, left: The control-rod runs of the engine controls. (A. Juszczak)

Above, right: The instrument panel seen from the right. (R. Pęczkowski)

Bottom, right: A close up shot of the main blind flying instruments. (R. Pęczkowski)

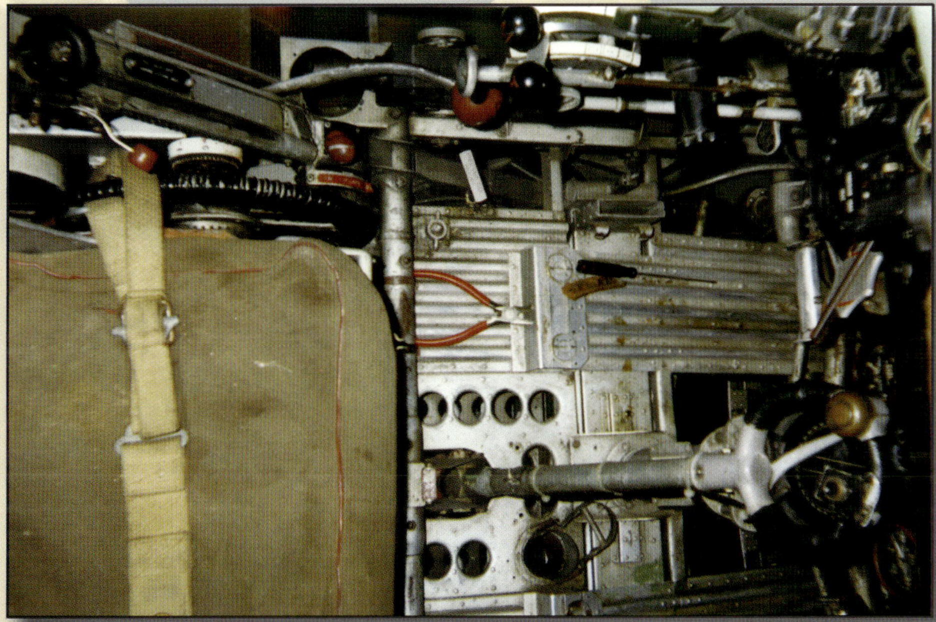

Above: The port side of the cockpit. The pilot seat is visible in the right.

Left: The cockpit from above, with the port side of the cockpit visible. Notice the absence of a 'floor' just heel guides. The control runs and arrangement from the control column are noteworthy. (Both R. Pęczkowski)

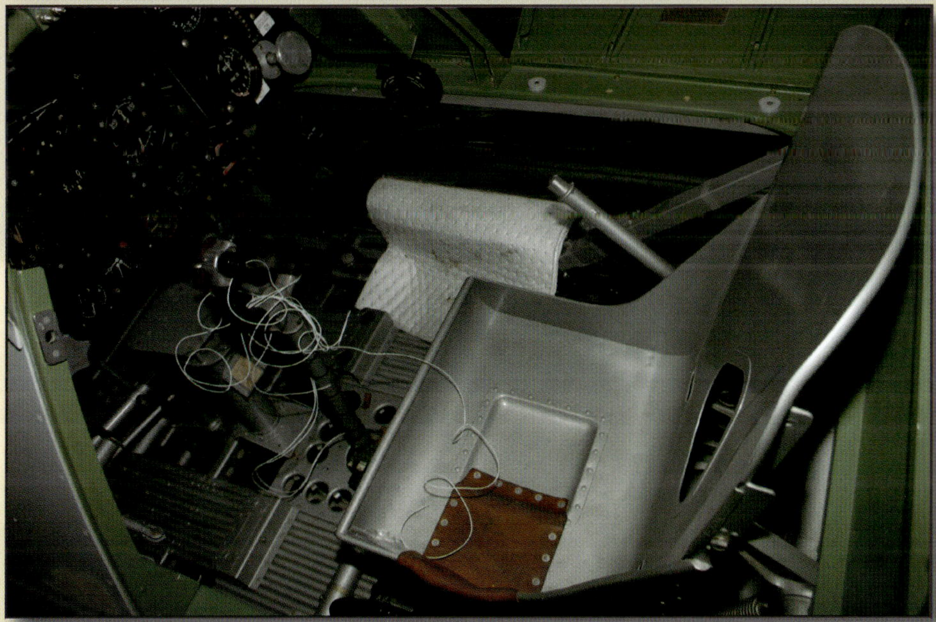

Another view of the he pilot seat and lower cockpit area during restoration. (A. Juszczak)

The starboard side of the cockpit, with the pilot's seat-height adjustment lever visible. (R. Pęczkowski)

The reflector gunsight used in the Gladiator.
(A. Juszczak & R. Pęczkowski)
Opposite and the next pages. *3D drawings of the cockpit details.*
(M. Ryś)

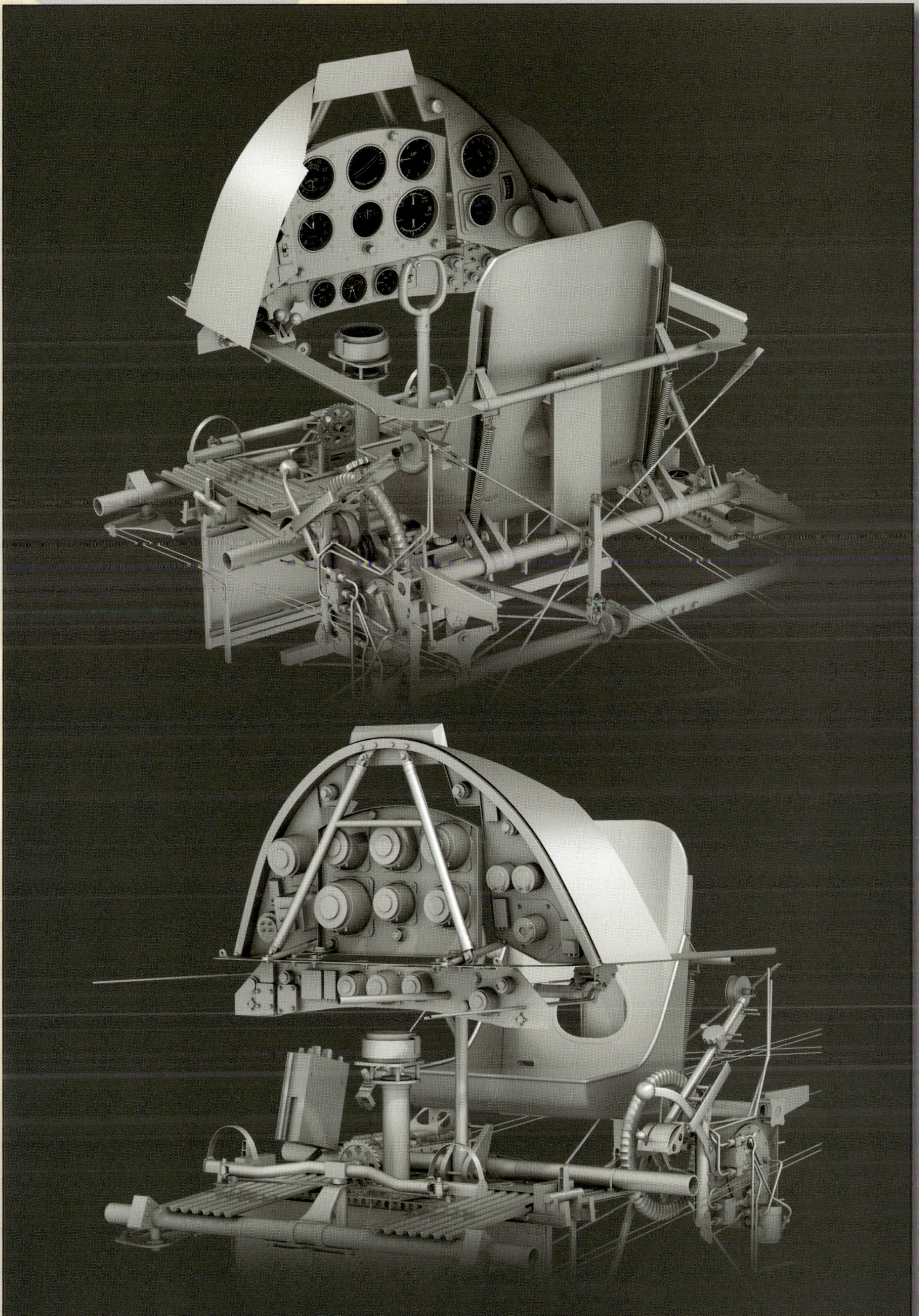

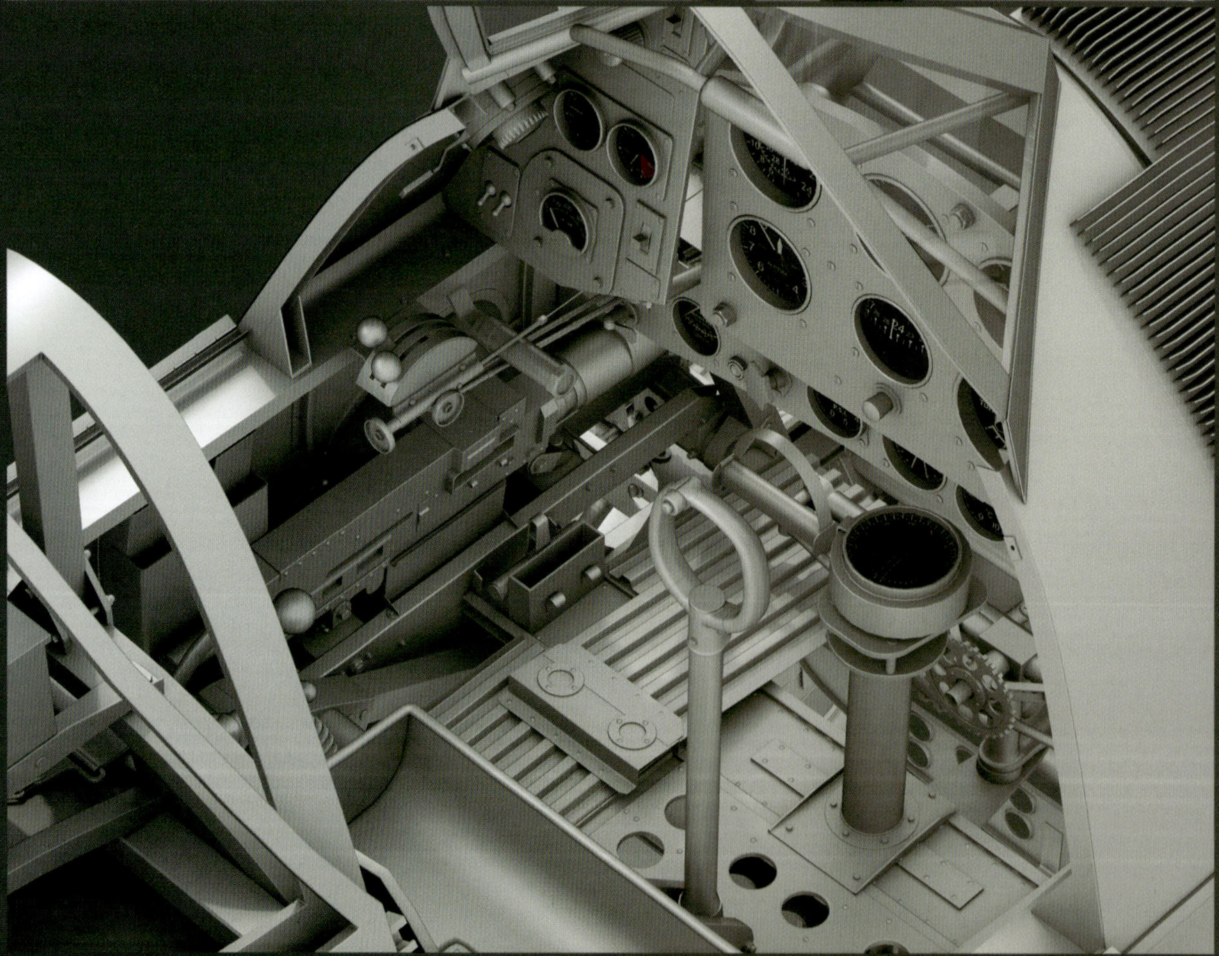

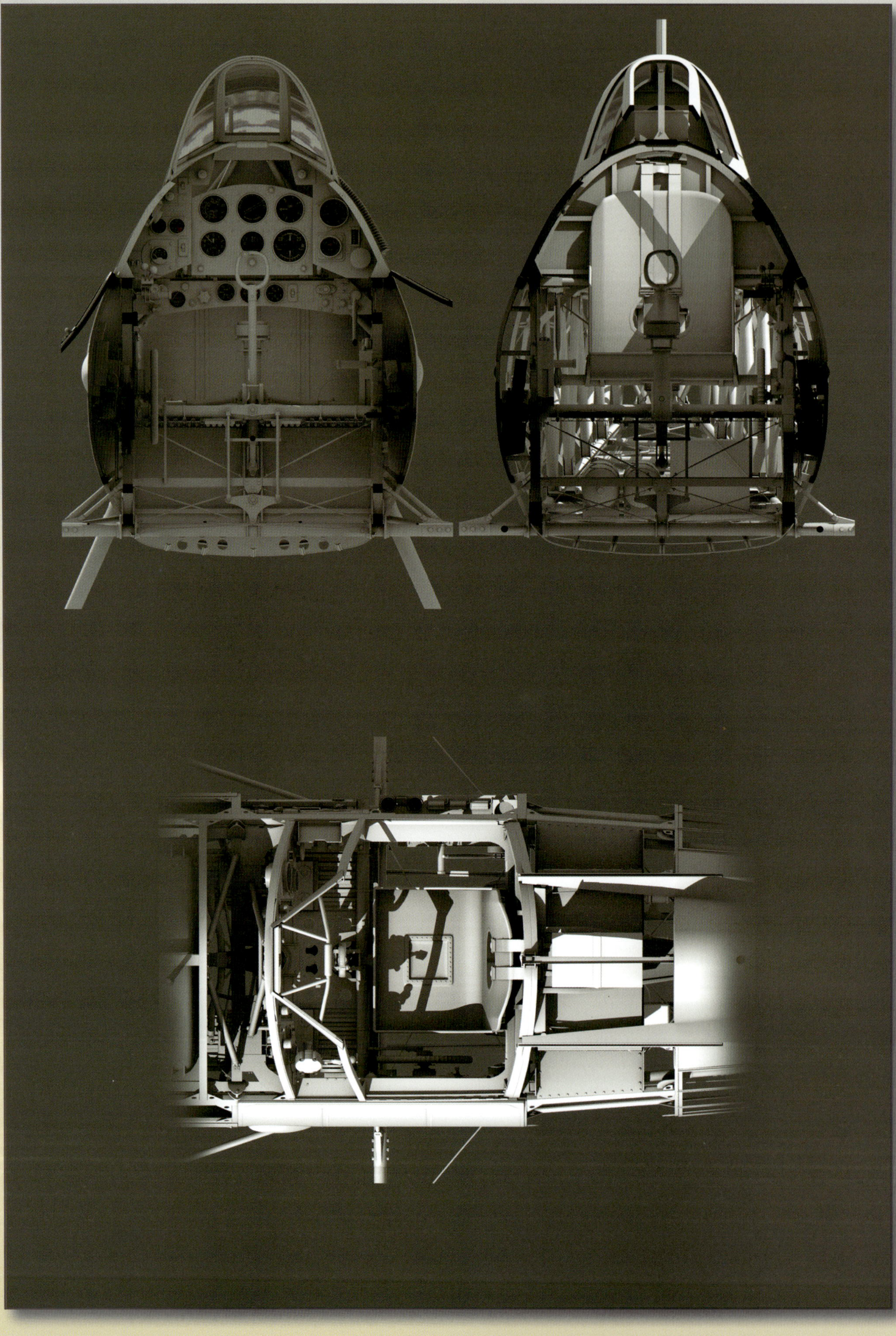

Above. 3D drawing of the pilot's seat arrangement. (M. Ryś)

Left: The starboard side of the cockpit with the access panel removed. The rear part of the machine gun, pilot's Sutton harness straps and seat are visible.

Below: Another view of the cockpit 'floor' area, with the lower part of the control column visible.
(Photos R. Pęczkowski)

Above: *Photos of the cockpit access doors in the open position. (A. Juszczak & R. Pęczkowski)*

Right: *two wartime photos of the captured Gladiator. Details of the cockpit access dors are visible. (Stratus coll.)*

Opposite page: *3D drawings of the Bristol Mercury engine. (M. Ryś)*

This page: *Engine and engine cowling details. (R. Pęczkowski)*

Opposite page, top: *3D drawings of the Mercury IX engine. (M. Ryś)*

Opposite page, bottom: *Three-quarter front view of the The Fighter Collection's Gladiator during restoration. (R. Pęczkowski)*

Above left: *The through-engine air intake. Engine details, cylinders, exhaust pipes and engine mounting* (**bottom photo**) *(A. Juszczak & R. Pęczkowski)*

Photos of the exhaust pipes and their mount. (R. Pęczkowski)

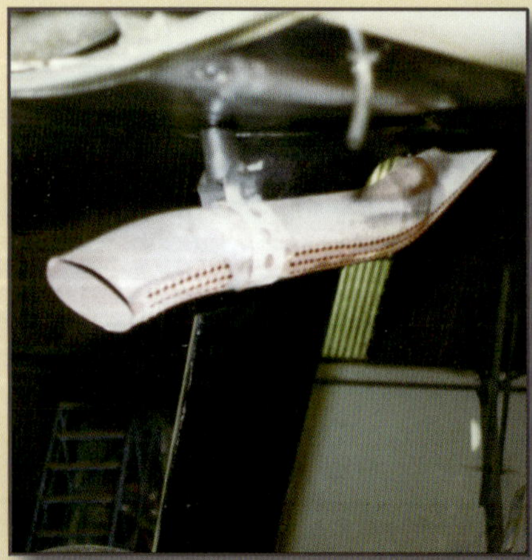

Four photos of the carburettor air intake. (A. Juszczak & R. Pęczkowski)

Below: Townend exhaust collector ring. (R. Pęczkowski)

Above and right: The fin and rudder seen from the right. Note the tailplane bracing wires. (R. Pęczkowski)

Port side of the rudder, with the rear navigation light also visible. (R. Pęczkowski)

Lower part of the rudder. Note the rear navigation lamp. (R. Pęczkowski)

Above: *Detail of the rear navigation light.*

Left: *Underside of the starboard tailplane and the elevator.*

Upper view of the tailplane. Bracing wires are clearly visible. Note the outline shape of the tailplane is clear here.

Rear part of the fuselage. Lower tailplane bracing wire is visible.
(Photos A. Juszczak & R. Pęczkowski)

Top: The Shuttleworth Gladiator touching down and showing the undercarriage arrangement. There is a degree of flex in the undercarriage legs, but the main suspension is in the patented Dowty hub. (A. Juszczak)

Left: Port mainwheel, inner view. (R. Pęczkowski)

Bottom: Port mainwheel and main leg from above. (A. Juszczak)

The mainwheel details; the Dowty internal-sprung shock-absorber is visible. (A. Juszczak)

Front view of the main undercarriage leg, The wide-angle lens distorts the alignment to the line of flight. (A. Juszczak)

The port mainwheel with cover fitted. (R. Pęczkowski)

Tailwheel, port side. (R. Pęczkowski)

Two photos of the tailwheel and its shock absorber. (Both A. Juszczak)

Above: *3D drawing of the Gladiator fuselage. Undercarriage with all covers removed.*
Below: *Details of the port machine gun. (Both M. Ryś)*

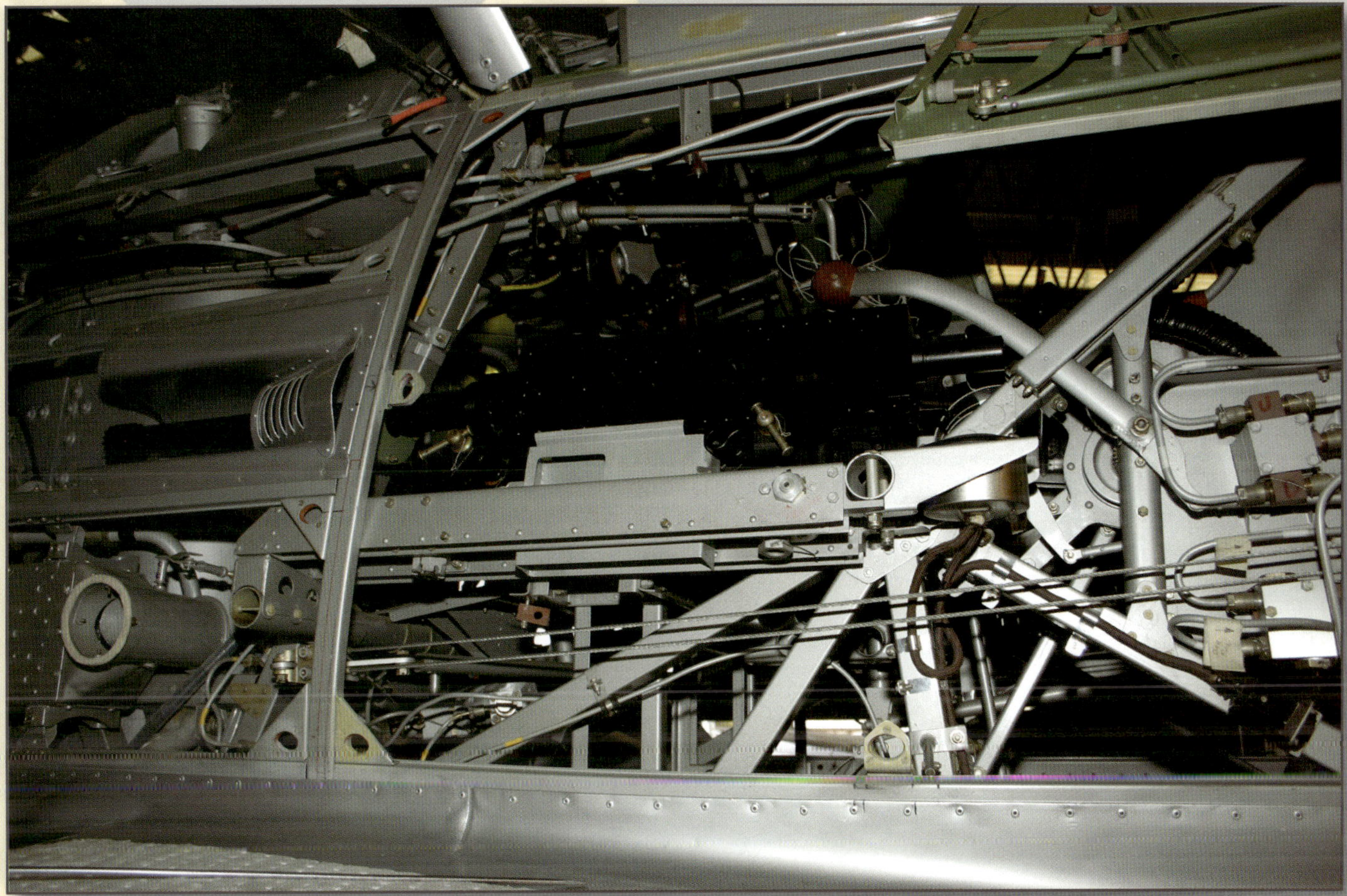

Above and left: The Colt Browing .303 machine gun as mounted in the Gladiator fuselage (A. Juszczak).

Bottom, left. The Browing .303 machine gun fitted through into the blast-trough. (R. Pęczkowski)

Bottom, right: Another view of the fuselage machine gun details. (A. Juszczak)

The fuselage mounted .303 Browing machine gun muzzle. (R. Pęczkowski)

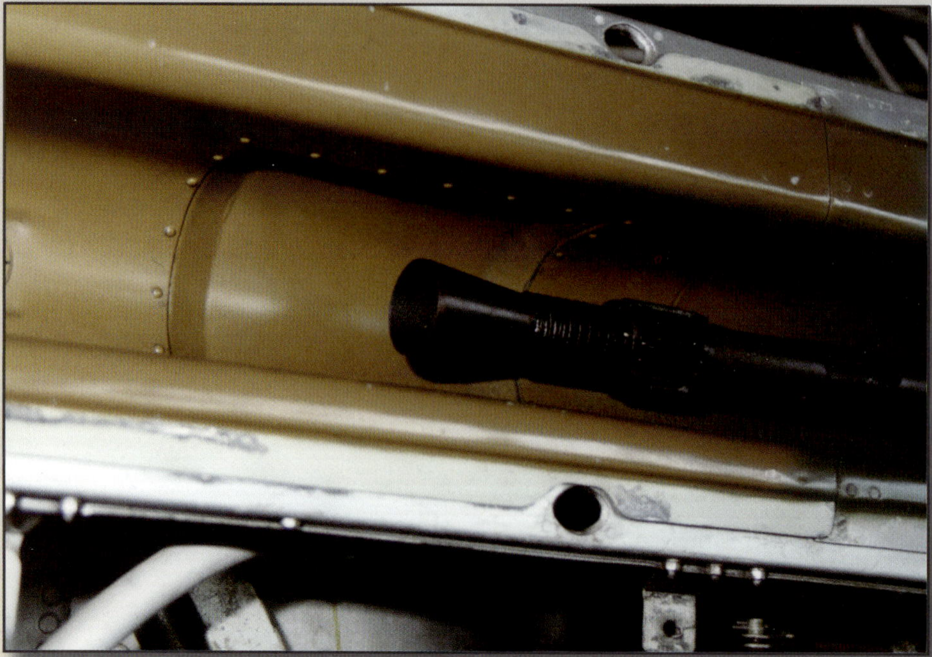

Another shot of the fuselage machine gun muzzle. (R. Pęczkowski)

Starboard side fuselage machine gun trough. (A. Juszczak)

Above: Underwing gun barrel and muzzle.

Left: The underwing gun muzzle.

The wing gun-bay with the Lewis .303 machine gun removed.
(All photos R. Pęczkowski)

The Gladiator makes a low pass and shows off the underwing Lewis .303 machine guns. (R. Pęczkowski)

Bottom: *A period photograph of the Sea Gladiator N5525, clearly showing the under wing machine guns and dinghy stowage between the undercarriage legs. The arrestor hook is also visible. (Stratus coll.)*

Swedish J8A in Detail

***Above:** Starboard side of the Gloster J8A Fv278 on show in the* Flygvapenmuseum *(Swedish Air Force Museum)* Linköping.

***Below:** Starboard side of the J8A fuselage. Note two machine gun fairings and Venturi tube just below the rear, central strut. (Both photos B. Belcarz)*

Port side of the engine cowling. Swedish style carburettor air intake is clearly visible.

Detail shot of the Swedish style carburettor air intake.

Port side of the J8A fuselage. Two teardrop machine gun fairings are visible. (All photos B. Belcarz)

Above: Two photos of the two-blade airscrew. Spinner is removed.

Rear wiew of the Engine cyliders. Starter crank is also visible. (All photos B. Belcarz)

Venturi tube at the port side. Details of the centre strut and bracing are visible.

Port side of the J8A tail. Tailplane bracing wires are visible. Note also sternpost and elevator hinges.

Starboard sternpost and control cables. Tailplane screw jack is also visible. (All photos B. Belcarz)

Main undercarriage of the Swedish J8A. (All photos B. Belcarz)

Photos showing details of the tail ski. (B. Belcarz)

To see stereo 3D drawings use attached glasses.

To see stereo 3D drawings use attached glasses.

To see stereo 3D drawings use attached glasses.

To see stereo 3D drawings use attached glasses.

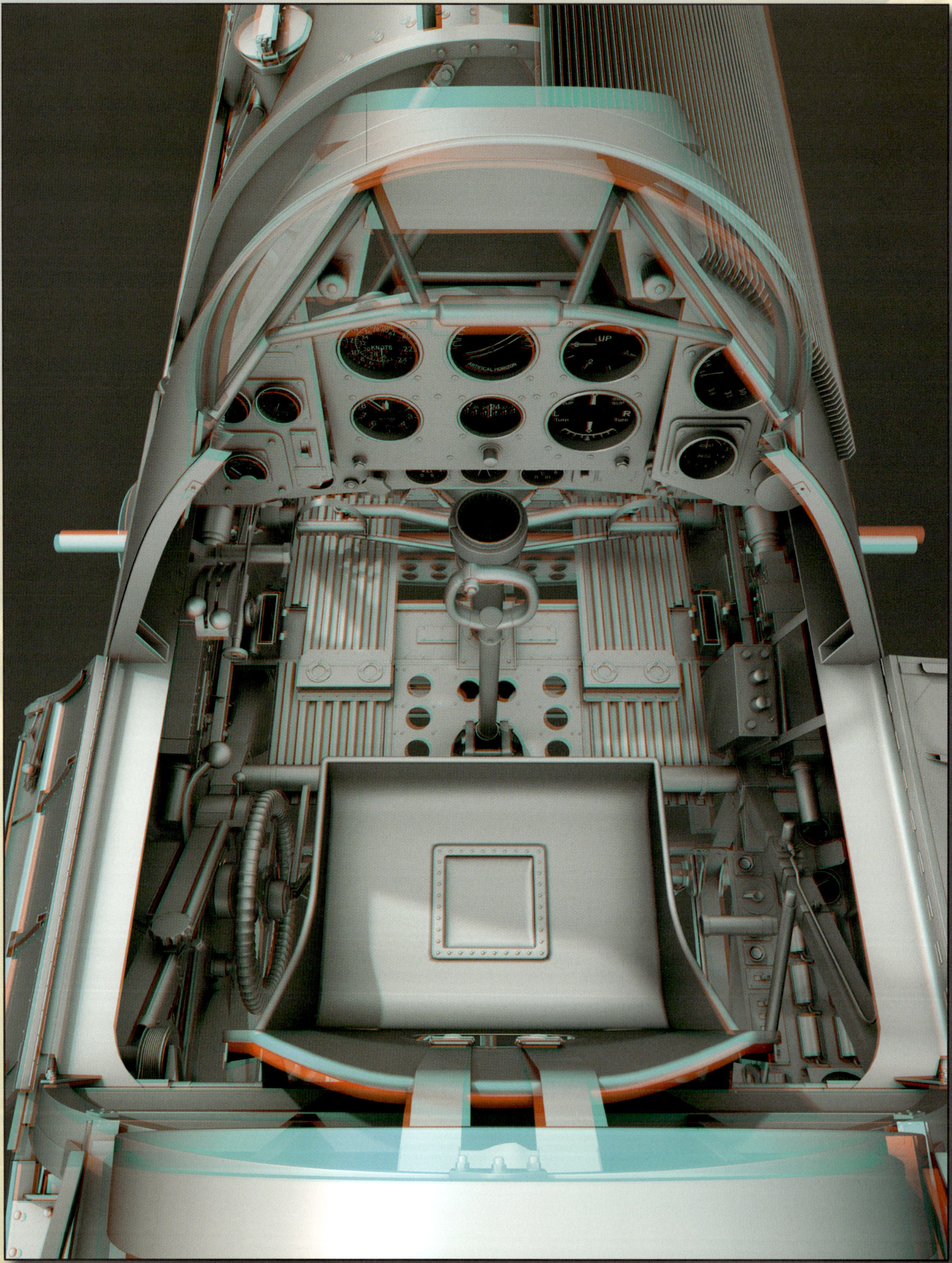

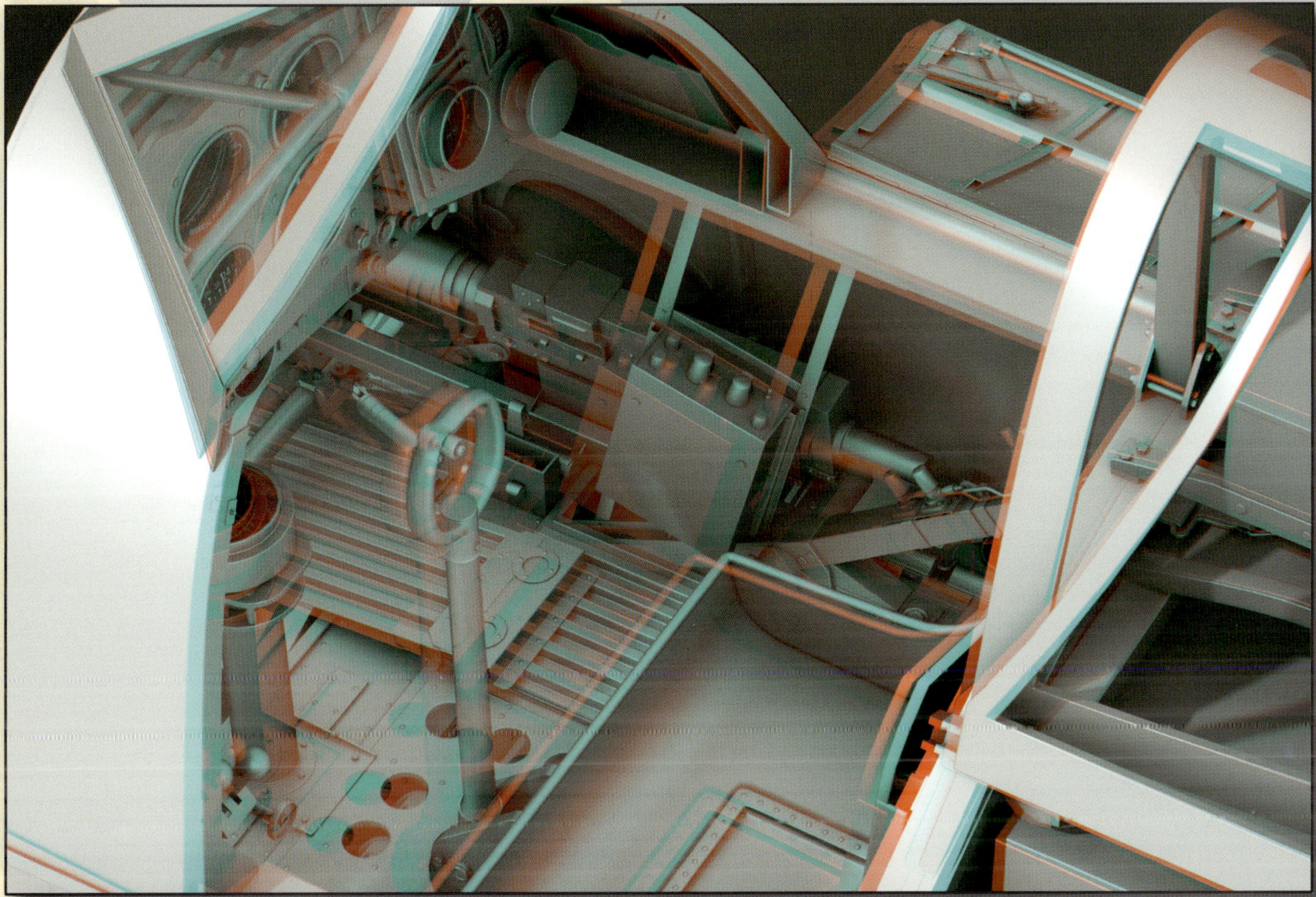

To see stereo 3D drawings use attached glasses.

Gloster Gladiator Mk I, K6150 of 3 Squadron RAF, Kenley, 1937-1938. Overall aluminium dope with roundels in all six positions. Serial in black on fuselage, rudder and lower wings. Squadron markings in green.

Gloster Gladiator camouflage & markings are described in detail in vol. I of this book.

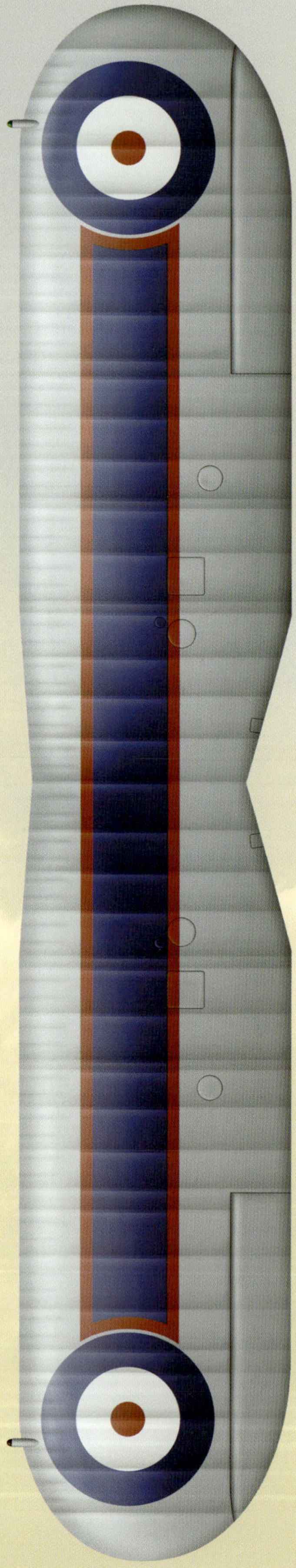

Both pages: *Gloster Gladiator Mk I, K6130 of 73 Squadron RAF, Church Fenton, 1937-1937. Overall aluminium dope with roundels in all six positions. Serial in black on fuselage, rudder and lower wings. Squadron markings – red/blue/red bars on fuselage and upper wing. Flight colours on the wheel covers, while the red fin and tailplane denote the Flight Commander's aircraft.*

K6130
K6130

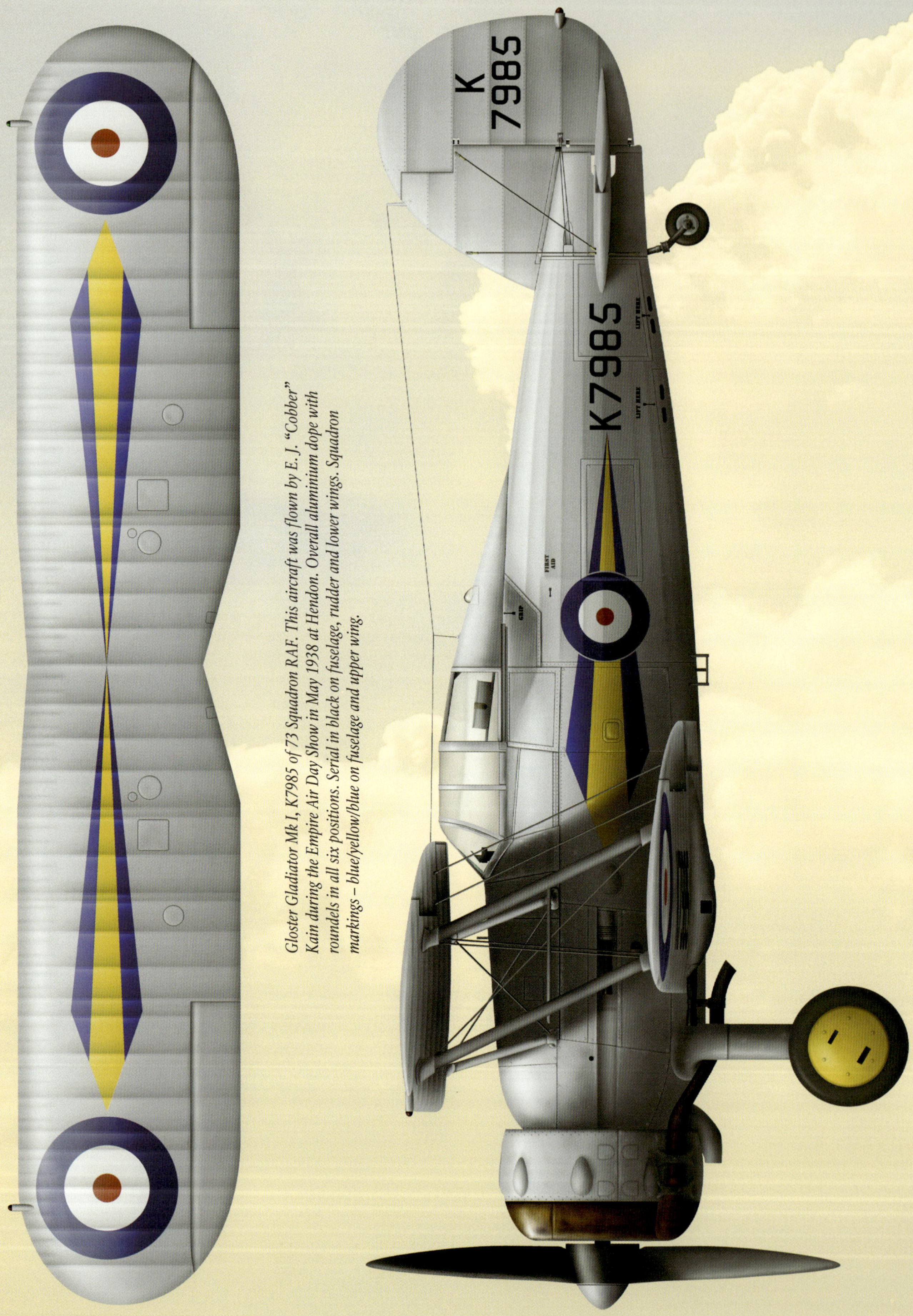

Gloster Gladiator Mk I, K7985 of 73 Squadron RAF. This aircraft was flown by E. J. "Cobber" Kain during the Empire Air Day Show in May 1938 at Hendon. Overall aluminium dope with roundels in all six positions. Serial in black on fuselage, rudder and lower wings. Squadron markings – blue/yellow/blue on fuselage and upper wing.

Gloster Gladiator Mk I, K6914 of 80 Squadron RAF, 1938. Overall aluminium dope with roundels in all six positions. Serial in black on fuselage, rudder and lower wings. Squadron badge on the fin.

Both pages: *Gloster Gladiator Mk I, K7974 of 87 Squadron RAF, 1938. Overall aluminium dope with roundels in all six positions. Serial in black on fuselage, rudder and lower wings. Squadron markings – light green/ black on fuselage and upper wing. Aircraft carries a 601 Squadron "Flying Sword" on the fin. Personal emblem (Popeye) on the starboard side of the fin.*

K7974
K
7974

K
7974

Both pages: *Gloster Gladiator Mk II, N7974, RT•O of 112 Squadron RAF, 1940. Dark Green and Dark Earth upper surfaces with Night undersurfaces. Roundels in all six positions. Serial in black on fuselage. Red wheel covers.*

Undersurace of Gloster Gladiator Mk II, K7974, RT•O of 112 Squadron RAF, 1940.

Gloster Gladiator Mk II, N2682, HP•K of 247 Squadron RAF, 1940. Flown by Sqn Ldr P.G. O'Brien. Dark Green and Dark Earth upper surfaces with Sky undersurfaces. Roundels in all six positions. Serial in black on fuselage. Red spinner and yellow wheel covers.

Both pages: *Gloster Gladiator Mk II, N2682, HP•K of 247 Squadron RAF, 1940*

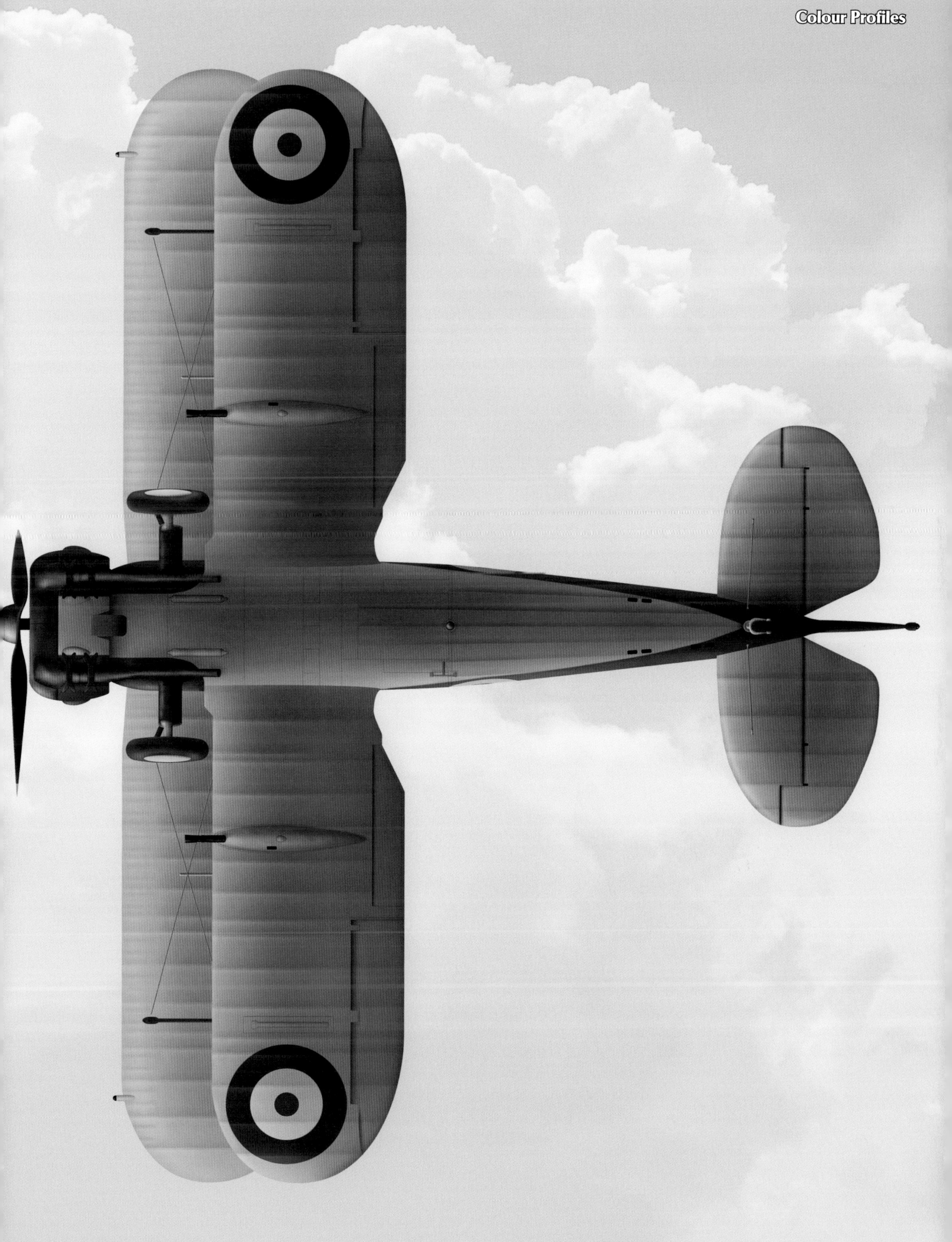

Both pages: *Gloster Gladiator Mk II, N5905, HE•N of 263 Squadron RAF, 1940. Dark Green and Dark Earth uppersurfaces with Night undersurfaces. Roundels in all six positions. Serial in black on fuselage.*

Gloster Gladiator Mk II, N5905, HE•N of 263 Squadron RAF, 1940.

Gloster Gladiator Mk I of Iraqi Air Force. Aircraft is in standard aluminium dope overall. Iraqi markings in six positions. Serial number is black and represents 202.

SAAF Gladiator No 1339. Aircraft Dark Green and Dark Earth upper surfaces with Sky undersurfaces. Wasp badge painted on the fuselage.

Gloster Gladiator Mk II, GL-264 of 2.LLv 26 Finnish Air Force, summer 1942. Olive Green and Black upper surfaces with Light Grey undersurfaces. Finnish national insignia in six positions. Serial – black. Yellow theatre indentification stripes. Silver crocodile on the rudder.

***Both pages**: Gloster Gladiator Mk II, GL-269 of of 1/LLv 26 Finnish Air Force, flown by Capt Paavo Berg (5 victories) , Utti, Finland, February 1940. Aircraft in Shadow Shading camouflage: Dark Green/Dark Earth plus Light Green/Light Earth on the parts of the aircraft that would be in the shadow, with Night-White undersurfaces. Finnish national insignia in six positions. More on the camouflage see vol. I.*

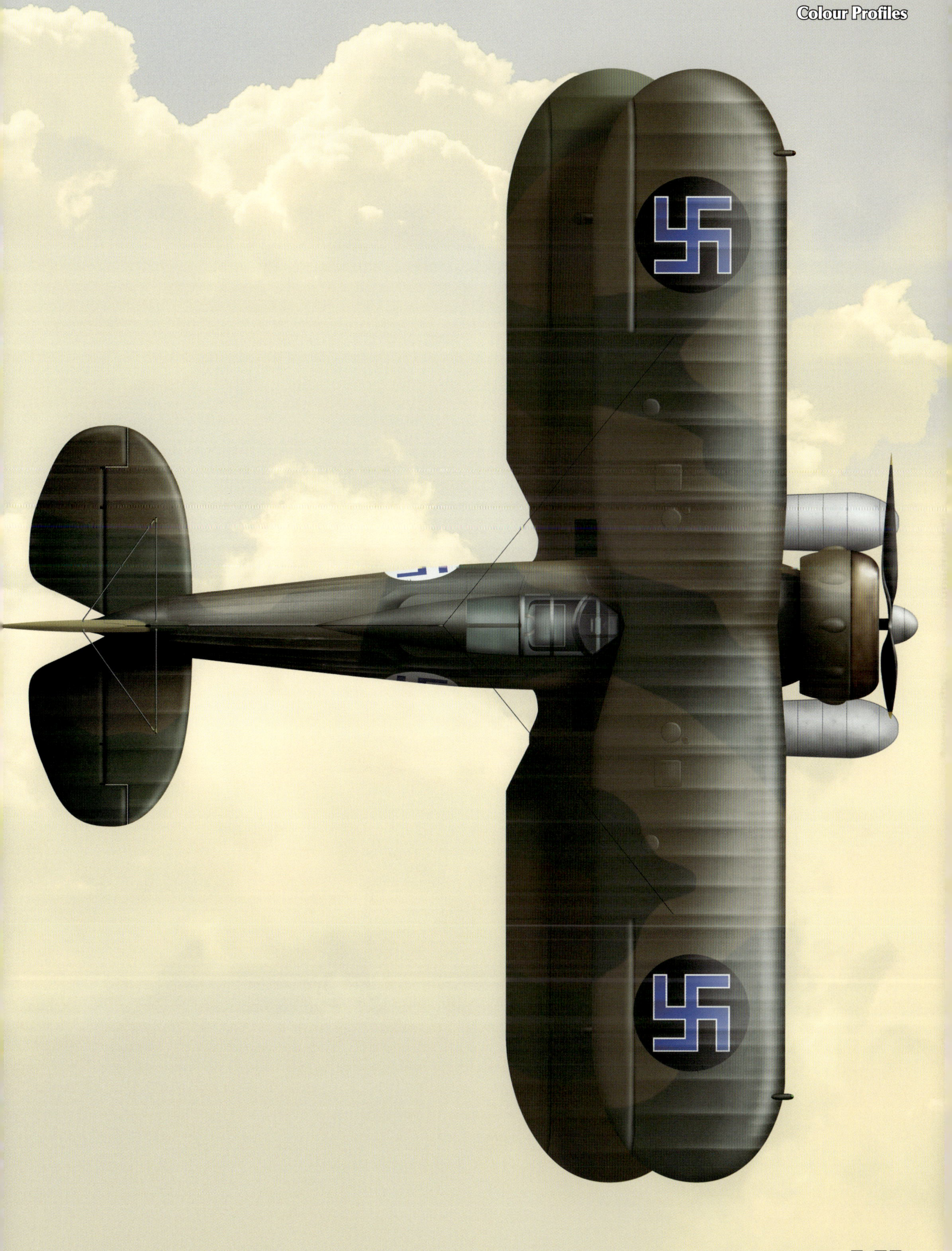

Gloster Gladiator Mk II, GL-269 of of 1/LLv 26 Finnish Air Force,

Gloster Gladiator Mk II, GL-273 of 1/LeLv 16, Finnish Air Force, 1941. Aircraft in Shadow Shading camouflage with Night-White undersurfaces. Finnish national insignia in six positions.

Both pages: *Gloster Gladiator Mk II, GL-273 of 1/LeLv 16, Finnish Air Force, 1941.*

273
GL –

Gloster Gladiator Mk II, GL-275 of 1/LeLv 16, Finnish Air Force, 1943. Aircraft in Green/White upper surfaces with Light Blue undersurfaces. Finnish national insignia in six positions.

Swedish J8 No. 231, F8-1, 1935. Aircraft aluminium dope overall with early Swedish national Markings.

Both pages: *Gloster J8A, No. 278, F8-48 of the Swedish Air Force, 1937. Upper surfaces olive green with light blue/grey undersurfaces. Swedish insignia* Kronmärke *without trim in six positions. This aircraft is now preserved at Swedish Air Force Museum.*

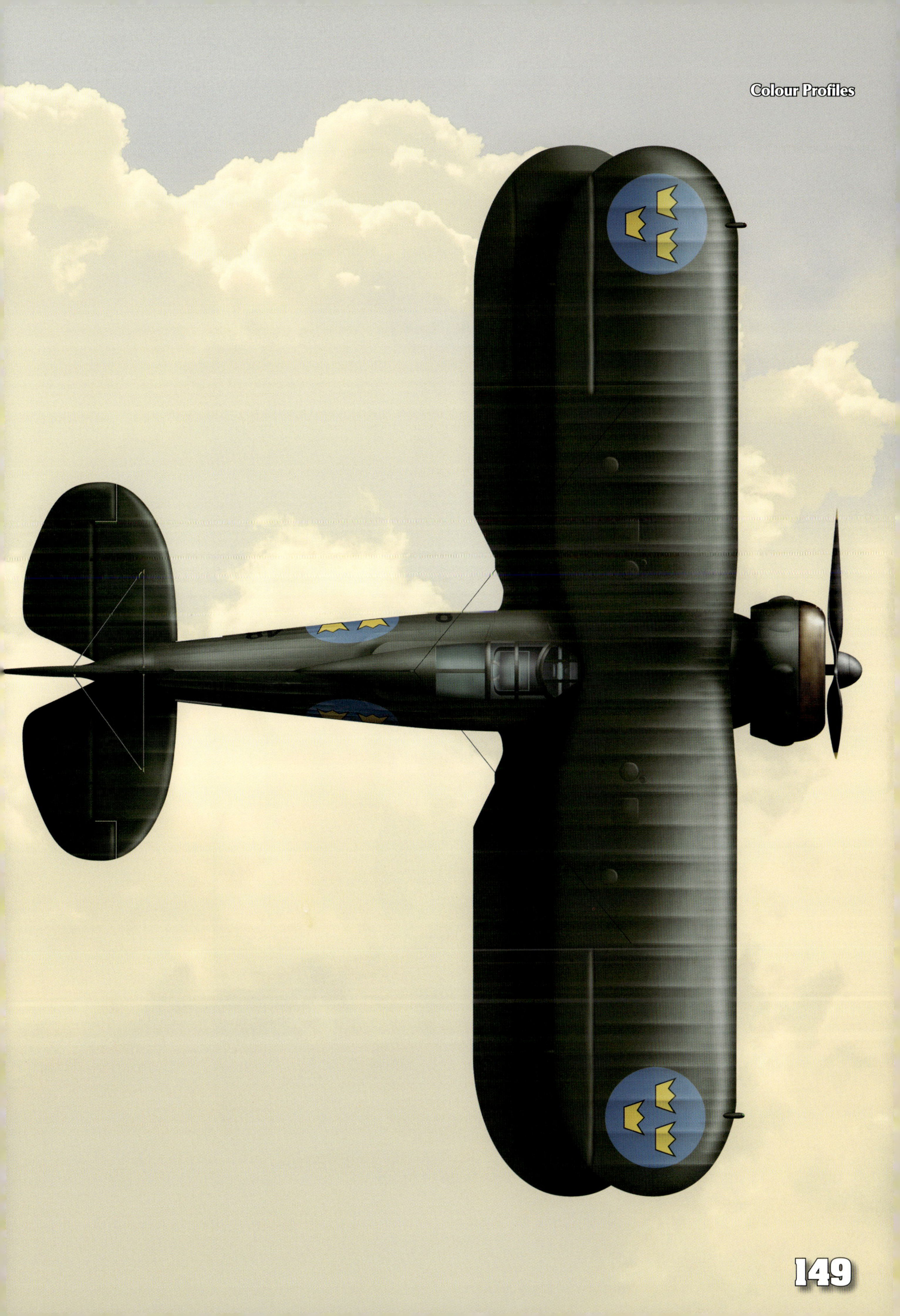

Swedish J8A. No. 279, 'G'of F19 after returning to Sweden. Aircraft in Swedish camouflage of Olive Green upper surfaces,Light blue/Grey undersurfaces overpainted with silver stripes.. Finnish national insignia, overpainted. Black/White Gandi and black skull and crossbones, seven kill markings.

Swedish J8A. No. 284, 'F' of F19, Finnland 1940, Winter War. Aircraft in Swedish camouflage of Olive Green upper surfaces,Light blue/Grey undersurfaces overpainted with silver stripes. Finnish national insignia on the fuselage and wing undersurfaces.

Both pages: *Swedish J8A. No. 284, 'F' of F19 after returnining to Sweden. Finnish National insignia overpainted. Black/white big skull and corssbones, white wing with blue border. Black 13, sickle ans star. No aircraft number on the fuselage. White skull and crossbones and white kill mark on the fin.*

Swedish J8A. No. 284, 'F' of F19 after returning to Sweden.

Gloster Sea Gladiator, N5519, "G6A" of 802 Squadron, HMS Glorious, 1939. Aluminium dope overall with yellow stripe and wheel hubs. Black fin.

Both pages: *Gloster Sea Gladiator, N5519, "G6A" of 802 Squadron, HMS* Glorious*, 1939.*

N5519
N5519

Both pages: *Gloster Sea Gladiator, N5519 of 261 Fighter Squadron FAA, Malta, August 1940. Pilot Sgt. Plt. Robertson. Aircraft in standard FAA Shadow Shading camouflage: Extra Dark Sea Grey/Dark Slate Grey - upper wing, upper fuselageand tailplane; Light Slate Grey/ Dark Sea Grey - lower wing. Sky Grey undersurfaces.*

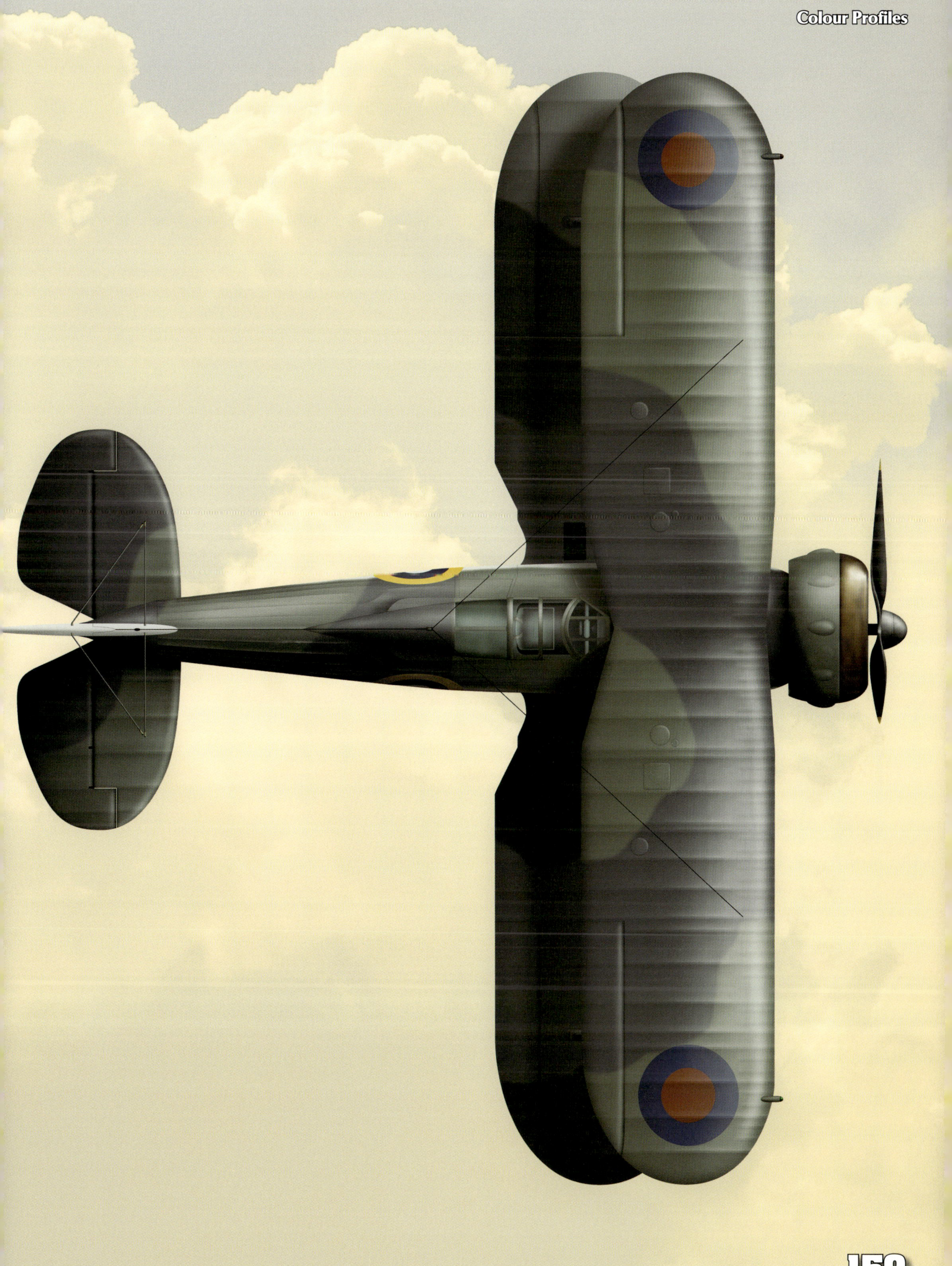

Gloster Sea Gladiator, N5519 of 261 Fighter Squadron FAA, Malta, August 1940.